MW01539572

Also by Thomas Farber

Fiction
The Beholder
A Lover's Question
Learning to Love It
Curves of Pursuit
Hazards to the Human Heart
Who Wrote the Book of Love?

Nonfiction
A Lover's Quarrel
Other Oceans (with Wayne Levin)
Provocations (with Robert Kuszek)
The Face of the Deep
Through a Liquid Mirror (with Wayne Levin)
On Water
Compared to What?
Too Soon to Tell
Rag Theatre (with Nacio Brown)
Tales for the Son of My Unborn Child

Epigrams
The Twoness of Oneness
Truth Be Told
Compressions: A Second Helping
The Price of the Ride

BRIEF NUDITY

BRIEF NUDITY

THOMAS FARBER

MĀNOA BOOKS ⚞ EL LEÓN LITERARY ARTS

HONOLULU / BERKELEY, CALIFORNIA

2009

Copyright © Thomas Farber 2009

No part of this book may be reproduced in any manner
without written consent from the publishers,
except in brief quotations used in reviews of the book.

Brief Nudity is published by
Mānoa Books
an imprint of The Mānoa Foundation
(www.themanoafoundation.org)

&

El León Literary Arts
(www.elleonliteraryarts.org)

Distributed by Small Press Distribution, Inc.
1341 Seventh Street
Berkeley, CA 94710
800-869-7553
www.spdbooks.org

ISBN 978-0-9795285-2-1
Library of Congress Control Number: 2008936929
Printed in the United States of America

Cover design and photograph by Andrea Young
Text design by Pat Matsueda

Note: The following text contains Adult Content (AC),
Adult Language (AL), and Brief Nudity (BN).

For myself and others

Had I found myself among those peoples who are said still to live under the strict liberty of Nature's primal laws, I can assure you I would most willingly have portrayed the writer's self whole, and wholly naked.

MICHEL DE MONTAIGNE

The cottage: not visible from the street—leafy magnolia, plum, cedar, and acacia intervening. But through the second of two fences and gates, there it is: white with blue shutters and trim, and small, 900 square feet. Gabled roof, unenclosed wooden eaves, bay window, clapboard siding, off-center entrance on the right. Inside, wood wainscoting, hardwood floors, brick fireplace. Elements of "rustic simplicity" with hints of the Swiss and the Japanese, amalgam the builder, a century ago, took from the ubiquitous Craftsman bungalows and Arts & Crafts cottages.

In this home, it's late in the day, half past four, Lagavulin single-malt/unsalted roasted almond/salsa nap time, and…the phone rings. Bob. Familiar, mutually agreeable short-notice invite: "Supper at 5?" The writer's old friend rises early, dines early, runs a construction business. Time and materials, no bids: he's skilled, trusted. As usual, Bob suggests Fat Apple's, venerable hamburger joint now nouvelled, though Jack Londoniana, uninterrogated, remains on the walls.

Bob's inevitable chicken Cesar salad, the writer's spinach salad. Organ recital: seventy-two, Bob may have cracked a rib, is popping Vicodin; more than a decade younger, the writer's shaken a chest infection. Mayhems, commiserations. The writer then asks Bob if he'd mind going over renovations he made on the writer's cottage back in the mid-1970s.

"This for the realtor?" Bob knows the writer's thinking of selling.

Not that he wants him to leave town: they go back to outlaw days in 1967, when much of the apparently essential and true was in the face of government lawlessness, deceit. It was all Che and Zorro, Butch Cassidy before Bolivia.

"Nope. Need it for a story."

"Ah." More than once, Bob's been alert to the writer's pursuit of naming. Fatherless from early childhood, except for an alcoholic glimpsed only rarely, in high school Bob came upon Thoreau and Emerson, made them his mentors, quotes them still. Happens also to know a great deal about, among other things, pre-Columbian art and Escher, appreciates the writer's interest in metaphor.

The cottage: *Where I Fell to Earth*. Book by Peter Conrad, title catching how unintended the writer's decisions about (resting) places have been, as well as the plummet which may be part of settling *down*. Back in 1975, it was Berkeley once again. Exhausted by years of the counterculture rootlessness then idealized as freedom—Greece, North Africa, California, New York City, Hawai'i, Oregon, Cambridge/the Berkshires/Nantucket—he abruptly craved the secure, secured. When beautiful, intrepid Katrin and the writer, completing their first year as a tribe of two, took possession of the cottage, they painted—she painted?—the coffee-brown walls white. The idea was to make the two small bedrooms, living room, and kitchen more spacious. Also, under the influence of psychedelics ingested by the truly wine-dark Mediterranean, the writer had imprinted on Cycladic whitewash.

The cottage had an attic, accessible through a hallway ceiling hatch. They'd stand on a stepladder, hoist themselves up and over, but then they—Katrin, probably—built a very sturdy ladder out of scrap lumber, rungs perhaps playfully not quite parallel. This post-Shaker hypotenuse stayed in the hallway, attic now guest bedroom (foam mattress on floor) and storage area for her quilting materials. Lots of clambering: funky, functional, post-hippie.

After a few years—cottage too small for their books, bird wings, treadle sewing machine, cats, sextant, shells, guitar, deer and bird skulls, IBM Selectric, stones from a beach in Ireland's Gaeltacht, piles of fabric, and flea market treasures—the writer consulted his friend Bob. Resourceful, strong as an ox, determinedly Outside The System, not long before Bob had ramrodded construction of a multilevel house in the hills, all poles, decks, and Bay vistas in the surrounding eucalyptus. Now he was back after camping on Jenner Beach, slabbing precious, otherwise lost burl from redwoods washed down the Russian River to the sea. Former philosophy student, genially pondering dharma ambiguities as he read *The Lazy Man's Guide to Enlightenment,* Bob had also made a trip to India and Nepal, seeker wandering through Buddhist poverty. (Sacred, profane: his boots contained a stash of hundred-dollar bills, so he was loath to shed them to enter the temples.) That day in '75 Bob came by the cottage, an off-the-books carpenter/contractor, this incarnation entailed driving a 1940s Ford flatbed, plum-colored "double-dorjes" painted on the yellow-green doors. Tibetan thunderbolts of spiritual realization flying low under the IRS radar.

The renovation. In the course of a month of brutal heat, Bob sealed the hallway hatch, then cut a large opening in the ceiling of one of the bedrooms to build a too-steep-for-code staircase ("nonconforming," city inspectors would have deemed it). "That entailed heading off the joists," Bob explains at Fat Apple's. As he must have explained thirty years earlier. "Joists are horizontal structural members, floor and ceiling, designed to carry both dead and live loads." Bob grinned. "*Dead* is, say, the roof itself; *live*, things like snow on the roof." The header, the writer (again?) learned, was the beam inserted to support the joists. That done, Bob "reframed" the north and south gables to put in windows, did the same for two large skylights, installed pink "batts" of insulation, sheet-rocked the ceiling, and built "pony walls with hinged cabinet doors." Pony walls. The two-by-fours framing them intercepted the roof rafters, cutting their span, which gave added support while creating accessible storage space.

Since it was beyond budget to raise the roof, at the peak of the ceiling Bob's improvements left standing headroom only. With the cottage's small scale and steep stairs, this gave a familiar sensation of being on shipboard—down on the Bay, Katrin and the writer were acquiring the skills to go cruising in their (incredibly funky) trimaran. So many counterculture status inversions still operant, the converted attic possessed a toke of reverse chic.

One could write a partial history of the writer's life the last three decades—age thirty to sixty—from the point of view of the lumbering, easily caught crane flies on, say, the downstairs bedroom wall. *Tipilidae oleracea* rematerialize late each winter, have wingspans of several inches, lose legs easily, bumble into the cottage not to eat but to mate in an adult life played out in a matter of days. (Since the writer has not tracked any one of them 24/7, he takes such data on faith.) Lord of this Manor, he's placed crane flies under his protection.

Here, however, our interest is not the downstairs bedroom but the storage space behind the studs ("vertical support members," Bob reminded him) of those pony walls. A year earlier, the writer concluded that to have any hope of moving from the cottage he had to cut down on his accumulations (Latin, *accumulatus*, "heaped up"). Back in the '70s, he'd finished a second book and written a third to the tintinnabulation of Katrin's finger cymbals as she belly danced in the living room. Though the writer then first acquired his trademark addiction to industrial ear protectors, readers will discern in his prose the doumbek's downbeats, the chattering zils. After Katrin and he separated in 1981, as he became ever more relentlessly a writer, the cottage began to reveal itself an artisan's workshop. Simple, spare furnishings. Order: a writer, he'd concluded, was someone who could find things. The bookshelves alone were teeming—sagas, data, personalities (authors; subjects), lost and imagined worlds, all the words in the writer's dictionaries/thesaurus/concordance. The cottage only looked bare.

Part of the writer's job seemed to be to keep things within reach but out of sight and mind. (Updike was the one author he read who called attention to the métier's requisite secretarial skills.) The writer's accountant had enjoined him to retain back tax data for five years against possible audits. Each April, in a mania of anxious approximation, the writer would channel numbers for self-employment deductions. (Always smaller than he could back up, it should be said; he was given a refund in his only audit.) Then he'd stuff the year's receipts—used manila envelopes Magic Marked PHONE, BOOKS, TRAVEL, MEDICAL—into a cardboard box to shove under the eaves. This annual sequestering, with gag reflex, went on for decades.

The impulse to purge, cleanse, rid, evacuate. Late in life, it amused the writer's mother-the-poet to use the verb *divest* to describe tax-deductible gifts to her four grown children. (Divest: Latin, *vestis*, "garment," hence undress, strip.) That week of the writer's supper with Bob, he invoked his mother's wordplay as he emailed family and friends to say he was divesting extra copies of her many books. Who wanted them? He then lugged twenty-odd boxes stored in the garage to the post office. Felt both relieved of a great weight and…rue. Acting as his mother's literary agent had been part of his writer's life. Just what was finished? On the other hand, mailing off these books—remaindered editions; copies held on to for promotion or gifts—sent him back to his remaining set. Rereading mother tongue. From a poem for children in *Small Wonders*:

> the ripest fruit of all:
> that star about to fall.

Writer himself a star perennially about to fall, he retained that set of his mother's many books. Not to mention her dozens of unpublished manuscripts; black-covered binder carefully listing decades of which periodical took which poem (more than a thousand published!); countless file cards with quotation noted. For instance, "Improvisation is adoration of the melody." Something the writer's mother made use of in her meditation on the death of the writer's father. And something, *pace Mater*, he could make use of. He remembers how crucial it was after his mother's death to be custodian of her papers, blesses his siblings for consenting. Beyond a no doubt Oedipal impulse to possess the body of his mother's work, he felt her papers, in toto, would confirm their bond despite so many struggles. Might explain how he too became a writer, for all the differences between them.

Sic Mom. Those hundreds of books of hers he shipped off had been in the garage. Also there, wedged up on a shelf with boxes of her papers, was a roll of maps and nautical charts. Point Reyes, Bar Harbor, Vitu Levu, Monterey to Coos Bay, Hilo, the Baja Peninsula, Rotuma, a great circle map of San Francisco to "all points on the earth's surface." For years, maps and charts enlarged the writer's spirit, helped him construe the world in terms of topography, soundings, elevations, archipelagos. Were also fictions that consoled, as if, about to depart from home once again, he could say where he was going. As if, having stepped off the path of the academic or professional life he'd expected to follow, he still had some sense of destination.

In that period of bearing his mother's books to the post office, the writer met a young woman, twenty-three, like Katrin a collector of thrift-shop treasures. Something pre-computer, pre-Internet, about her. No cell phone: very appealing. Besides the savor of apparent anachronism, he was drawn to her because, during their first conversation, despite her wit and verve she suddenly faltered. She'd recently been broken up with by her lover. "Dumped," as she put it. Sometimes, with a stranger, one has an instant of unexpected clarity, empathy. This stranger also could give a mischievous look that triggered affectionate recollection: filmmaker he'd been with briefly, decades before, just prior to meeting Katrin. The filmmaker had told him she was trying to decide between two boyfriends, was emotionally exhausted, couldn't start anything else. This at one in the morning: they'd just seen Bertolucci's *Last Tango in Paris*. Then that mischievous look, and so to bed. Each of these human echoes, and the young woman's enthusiasm for the maps as they dusted off spiderwebs, made them hers. The writer felt no regret giving her an 1851 chart of the world's whale populations.

But the charts and maps had also been in the garage. As for the writer's resolve to deal with the contents of the cottage, where to begin? The previous two years, he'd been visited by no fewer than three—let us not understate—*plagues*. One was all too familiar: early winter flu (despite or because of his annual flu shot), euphemism for exhaustion/depression/immobility, interminable days upstairs on the double bed. The writer's never figured out his relationship to these flus. Has thought of them as occasioned by the body's insistence on slowing him down; genetic flaw; character flaw; urban poison; something he ate, didn't eat; electromagnetic fields; bad karma; something to do with the cottage. These "flus" always stay far, far longer with him than with other people he knows, until, as if at long last tiring of the game, in their own sweet time departing. Worse, they seem to have a gift for remaining indecipherable; over the years, back when the writer still tried to at least name what was going on, nothing was ever revealed by this medical test or that. Well, not quite nothing: an acupuncturist once explained his *chi* was depleted. True enough. After needles and herbs failed to do the job, she passed her hands over him to transmit energy. Writer both consoled and mildly embarrassed for her.

Always with these flus, finally one day he wakes as out of a dream, finds himself restored to what he's never stopped defining, evidence to the contrary, as his "real" state of high vitality and exuberance. His OPB—Otherwise Perfect Body. Each flu leaves behind, however, the shadow of awareness that it can return if and as it wants, also knowledge that he's been forced to accede to it, even, surrendering, made complicit.

A good patient, the writer is not. Lying there one endless afternoon, he notices a black house fly *(Musca domestica)* out of season. Hauls himself back up the stairs from his next trip to the bathroom carrying a fly swatter. Locates the intruder, whacks it. But then he sees another, very large with a glistening sheen (German, *schoen*, beautiful). Though right-handed, he takes a swing lefty, like Ted Williams, baseball icon of the writer's Boston childhood. Fastidiously collects corpses with a Kleenex, takes them down to the garbage can. Sick as he is, a warrior's aim has been true. Male, depleted, in perennial hero narrative.

The next afternoon, upstairs on the bed to watch a DVD, he's dismayed to see more flies. Five or six. Again the swatter. Nearly each intemperate stroke, however, leaves another smudge on Bob's white sheet-rocked ceiling. Then, losing his temper, with a fierce blow the writer cracks a window on which a fly arrogantly stationed itself (or, he has to concede, just paused to contemplate the front yard or its navel). Worse, an aspect of the flu is enhanced self-pity: he hears himself moaning, "What have I done to deserve this."

Long story short, the writer acquired several more swatters, including one the size of a handball racquet. The infestation (Latin, *infestare*, "to assail or molest," hence "to haunt…in a troublesome manner") went on for two eternities. Two weeks. An apparently limitless supply of robust, shining young flies sallied forth from cracks around the exposed brick chimney like white-scarved young pilots in the Battle of Britain—but wait, the writer was defending *his* homeland. Though he had to admire how they glided "wimpling on a wing" (Gerard Manley Hopkins, one of his mother's favorites, talkin' windhovers), in the end, appreciating their grace as he analyzed flight patterns, feeling he knew their movements as well as they did, he snuffed out the light of life in every last one.

Thus the second plague. Meanwhile, regarding self-pity, the writer knew it was inappropriate. Months before, he'd heard something move around noisily in the attic walls, as if resituating furniture, heavy-footed scurrying. This happened repeatedly, even after he banged on the wall with his fist, slammed the cabinet door to drive The Whatever(s) away, so tearing out a hinge. Not mouse, not squirrel/raccoon/ant army/bird/marauding feline/possum/skunk, all of which over the years had entered the cottage. And surely not the butterflies/bees/moths/spiders he'd safely guided out of the cottage so many times. Whose testimony the writer counted on to help him avoid being turned on a spit over burning coals for ever and ever.

But now, hackles raised, he was loath to name the phenomenon, in a kind of trance returned from the hardware store with an "ultrasound" device. The package copy averred it would neither disturb humans nor interfere with TV reception, but would drive pests—if one can summarize—batshit. Inserted in the outlet, the device blinked, giving it an air of high-tech authority and victimless crimes (think Defense Secretary MacNamara's eyeglasses, circa 1967, bombers dropping slow-mo flowers over Vietnam). In fact, the next few months the ultrasound seemed to work. But then one late afternoon, as the writer lay on the upstairs bed watching a DVD of *The Deer Hunter*—incredibly young DeNiro, incredibly young Christopher Walken—sipping his daily Lagavulin single malt and munching roasted almonds, unsalted, again came the sound of something in the eaves. Something for sure the writer didn't want in the cottage. The writer, as before, pounded on the wall. More heavy-footed movement. "Not in my house!" he shouted. ("War" [grunt], Edwin Starr's Motown anthem begins, "What is it good for. Absolutely nothing.")

Back to the hardware store. The writer returned with "bait pellets" and "bait bits" he scattered in the corners of the eaves as if…as if broadcasting seed. For a millisecond Katrin's prescient fear of pesticides reached the writer's conscious mind, then vanished.

Painful memory. Katrin and the writer had come to struggle over, among other things, Agent Orange, though part of their initial affection was shared exultation in J.A. Baker's *The Peregrine*, threnody for the dying off of falcons, screed against DDT. Selective Luddites, seeing in California urban life not Jane Jacobs's neighborhood vitality but human despoliation, during their frequent wanderings they spent many months in sheep-and-cattle country. Yet another diner in yet another hamlet, something hyper-real in these as-if-evacuated towns, each building and remaining individual warranting, requiring special attention. Another thrift shop in the midday heat, Katrin poring over old clothes and art deco jewelry, writer checking the bookracks. Ah, worn paperback of Edward Abbey's *The Brave Cowboy*. But whereas on ranches the writer could celebrate the richness of rural traditions while cataloguing brutalities and paranoias—the authentic!—Katrin, truly gifted with animals (dogs, cattle, sheep, horses) came to see only careless overuse of chemicals, blighted landscape. Came to find the whole enterprise misguided. Perhaps, feeling the writer's life a trapeze act, he had a great stake in harnessing apprehension. Katrin, he…feared, had too much invested in an imagining of worst cases without corrective action. Nonredemptive story, he might have called it, as if his own stories redeemed things. (*Redeem*: to buy back, recover something pledged, make amends, restore from captivity by paying ransom. *Redeem* and *ransom,* it turns out, have the same Latin root.) Maybe, however, the writer was simply killing the messenger. Or, as Confucius never said, once you and your lover argue about Agent Orange, you're long since arguing about something else.

Whatever that millisecond of memory about Katrin, the writer broadcast the bait, neglecting to consider what could happen if some varmint (cowboy for vermin?) expired in there. Decay/putrefaction/rot. *De*composition in a cottage dedicated to composition. Thus the Jobean synchronicity of flu and the plague of flies. (Jobean, except that Job did not set in the motion the wager between God and The Adversary that occasioned his trials.) Then, a year later, the writer could no longer fail to acknowledge the small, hard, black, seed-like pellets on the attic floor. The Whatever(s) and the writer were not finished with each other. Back to the hardware store. Ten glue traps. But the traps stayed empty, and, after each weekly vacuuming by the writer's cleaning person, more droppings. Depleted by winter, he temporized.

The third plague. One evening, coming quickly through the gate at dusk, home from his seminar at the university, a graduate student having again prefaced scathing critiques of other students' work with, "As a queer Cambodian-American woman," the writer laughed to think of explaining to her that story told so insistently creates counterstory, that he could no longer believe she was queer, Cambodian-American, or a woman. Chuckling, though aware that if he told this anecdote it too might be called into question, the writer was then reawakened to the idiom, "He could not believe his eyes." A large…RAT…RACING up the side of the cottage on the cable TV wire? Disappearing under the eaves? Into the cottage? FUCK. SHIT. Unlocking the front door, dropping the satchel of student stories, he grabbed the Yellow Pages, thumbed to PEST CONTROL SERVICES, which, bless the ancient Sumerians (for the alphabet) and the writer's mother and the writer's public school education (for teaching him the alphabet), was there between PERSONNEL CONSULTANTS and PET BOARDING. Competitors included Rat Patrol, Keep 'Em Away, Home-team Pest Defense, and Critter Control. Terminex promised "The Complete Solution," a deafness-for-historical-echo which won the writer over. When the "technician" arrived the next morning, radiating good cheer—soon to go into exterminating on his own—he produced old-school traps baited with peanut butter.

Within days there were three gray corpses. "All gone," the technician said, though the writer remembered Camus' *The Plague*, as a college freshman confirmed and so cheered by its insinuation the bad times would inevitably recur.

"All gone." This telling makes light of the rat episode, but in truth it was them or the writer. As mentioned, he'd endeavored over the years to save or free many creatures that entered the cottage, and in the ocean, he'd often been down at one hundred feet within easy reach of scores of sharks, acknowledged they fairly had a claim on him. But rats? Like the flies, their presence spoke to him of being displaced. Of death. And death, he was insisting, was for outside the cottage. This though one of Katrin's cats, Ariel, was put down in the living room by the vet, Ariel part of the family. (A merciful acceleration he and his siblings had failed to provide their mother…)

With the attic's recent karma, then, the writer was resolved to clear out the many boxes of back tax documents under the eaves, an apparently imperative step toward the possibility of moving from the cottage, CHANGING MY LIFE, a phrase which now occurred to him in caps. Squatting before Bob's cabinet door, wearing carpenter's knee-pads—a sculptor friend referred to his set as "Lewinskis"—the writer peered in. So many boxes! And then the writer heard his interior monologue. One word. Another. True to his vocation, he got up, went downstairs to the dictionary. Still wearing kneepads, confirmed the mantle (cloak or cover) in dismantle, the literate in obliterate. Which was, no surprise, a "rendering indecipherable of writing or marks."

Again upstairs, on his Lewinskis in the far corner of the eaves, the writer pulled out a box marked 1991 from among the dried rat droppings. Reaching in, he extracted a pack of checks. 9/9/91, #1826, $100.00 to the State of Hawai'i, Harbor Division, Department of Transportation. Amazing: now he remembered. He'd once thought of living on a boat at Ala Wai Harbor in Honolulu. Problem was, you needed a berth, and there was a waiting list, annual fee to stay on it. Which he'd paid for a number of years until giving up—more than one owner of a live-aboard at Ala Wai insisted the list was rigged.

Old grievance. Forget it. The writer shook his head, leafed to check #1812, 9/1/91, $229.62, to Auto Tops + Interiors. For upholstery, he'd noted in red ink. That had to be the '78 Camaro, the writer's silver muscle car. Which, in 1997, he sent into an 180-degree spin in rush-hour traffic, then reluctantly donated to a charity which would get rid of it. Moving up to an '88 silver Accura Legend with disc brakes.

Well, if only to the writer, this was rich stuff, but, wow, slow going. He reached into another box. There was his 1983 Day-at-a-Glance Academic/Fiscal Planner, black, spiral bound. 1983. Rang no particular bells. He leafed through the months. Ah, right, it was in fact a 1983–84 calendar. Nineteen eighty-four: year the writer's mother died. Now, two decades later, the planner's entries were drenched in dramatic irony. Dramatic irony: term the writer learned back in high school. *Oedipus Rex.* Sophocles' king is earnestly looking all over Thebes for who's causing the problem. But the audience, watching him, well knows what he doesn't. The writer saw a summer production at Wellesley College when he was sixteen. Outdoor amphitheatre, masked young women the actors. Horrifying, when Oedipus comes back onstage having blinded himself.

So it's late 1983. The writer's visiting New York City, juggling appointments with women he's loved and women with whom he's now having affairs, at thirty-nine in a period of what he refers to as raging bachelorhood. This after the years with Katrin, the shelter and struggle of that bond and joint enterprise, followed by his determination to separate. Inexorable, but with regret, guilt. Still, he'd lost faith in the idea of them, together.

In New York at this particular moment, the writer's seeing editors and agent, has a fifth book forthcoming, is scheduling consulting work for foundations. And though it's not marked in the planner, he's about to get a call from a sibling saying his mother has had a brainstem stroke, that she's in Mount Auburn Hospital, that she must have been down on the floor of her apartment for many hours before she was found. Too much: the writer puts the planner in the box, backs out through the cabinet door, un-Velcros the Lewinskis.

Repetition compulsion. The writer's curiosity drives him back toward the boxes, but this time he's stopped at the pony walls. More words have come to mind. Again down to the dictionaries. *Excavate* (cavity, cave). *Disinter* (*terra*, earth). *Demise,* noun and verb: to dismiss; conveyance

of an estate; "decease of a royal or princely person, hence, grandilo-
quently, the death of a person…" And there is *re*demise, noun and
verb, which makes the writer smile. Who would'a thought?

The writer mulls the boxes under the eaves. Weird. For instance,
now it seems he mustn't allow himself to just throw the stuff in trash
bags and chuck it. Multi-talented Bob, undaunted by building or
fixing anything, has a part of his soul that unsettles and/or composes itself with thinking about that which he can't master. Failure of
the world banking system; meteorites; earthquake soil liquefaction.
News that twenty-six percent of Americans have a frontal lobe de-
formity making them—like the writer, baseball bat in his back seat,
Bob observes—prone to road rage. It's this Bob who tells the writer
he has to shred back tax data to prevent identity theft.

"Fuck it," the writer responds. "I'm worn out trying to be me. Let
somebody else give it a shot. As President Bush No. 2 nobly put it,
'Bring 'em on.'"

Bob nods. Meaning, "No."

As for keeping the boxes, what's in there, really? The writer could
spend the rest of his days sifting through receipt layers, his private
Grand Canyon, become his own garbologist. Think of grieving Orpheo in *Black Orpheus* (seen with the writer's high school girlfriend
in 1960, both of them teary-eyed, at Symphony Cinema in Back Bay,
hard by the Museum of Fine Arts/Symphony Hall/Jordan Hall/dog
training school for his family's hapless boxer). Orpheo searching for
lost Eurydice at the hall of records, as if she could be found in the
windblown paperwork.

But despite the writer's resistance to looking through the boxes,
to destroy possibly essential documents also threatens. Yet how is it

that this detritus (Latin, a rubbing away, hence disintegrated material, and the *i* is long, the writer reminds himself)...how is it that this debris (French, *briser*, to break, hence rubbish, fragments—see *bruise*) presents itself as "possibly essential"? Well, as regards the writer's own "mind," putting distance between it and his "self," he's leery of the tropes of his memory, paths it's used to. Is afraid of the formulae, actually, feeling the truth of the past is misrepresented. A given specific, "he" thinks, may reawaken—force—a truer narrative. Sometimes the writer feels like a lawyer impeaching his own witness, calling into question his own testimony. Thus daily journaling, never reread, comprising a skeleton transcript against which his own subsequent "art" could be measured.

Or can it? Even specifics have to lead somewhere, to story, and there are far too many specifics under the eaves. For the writer, to take them on turns out to be more like a foray: into the box, grab something, get out quick. *Foray*, from the Middle English, "to ravage in search of plunder." You ask, does the writer really believe memory is so fraught? Well, perhaps we all have to (re)examine our favorite stories. Or least favorite stories. See what, as the phrase goes, they've gotten us into.

But the cottage, the writer's factory. He's endeavoring to clear it. "You must change your life": Rilke's famous admonition, though there's little reason to think Rilke changed his. Still, the writer enjoins himself to try. And there's another factor. At sixty-one ("I am now sixty-one, sixty-two, sixty-three," Max Frisch's protagonist says in *Montauk*), the writer's finding it harder not to see that his life will end; when he's gone, someone will have to deal with what he hasn't taken care of. The writer has an acquaintance who for years let his house become ever more decrepit, a decades-long rage at where he'd ended up, despairing correlative of the disintegrating self. In his seventies, rewriting his will, this man laughed to explain he was bequeathing his house to a nephew who'd have to do what he himself could not, that is, clear out his memorabilia, papers.

What's left behind. As the writer and his siblings emptied their mother's apartment twenty years before, it began to dawn on him they were encountering only her public self. Business correspondence; manuscripts suitable for publication. Nothing intemperate, unseemly, private. Not a single love letter, even from their father? No journal from bitter adolescence, embattled middle age? Quite a feat for an aging senior, to have gotten rid of it, if that's what she did. Which she was surely capable of. Or, more likely, to have gotten free of it in the first place by preemptive transmutation into high art. More like transubstantiation, actually, exalted self's body and blood into art's wine and wafer. Or perhaps the writer's mother's life and thoughts were ever exemplary, occurred to her pre-transubstantiated? True, she could be relentlessly high minded. But still one believes literary types have uncooked thoughts on some piece of paper they are adverse to having others read. Well, not so with the writer's mother, if that's what he expected, feared finding. Which of course said something about his own back pages.

Think of Meher Baba, popular sixties avatar, whose "Just love me" was surely a line the writer ran by one woman or another without being taken for a deity manifested as human. Meher Baba? Or Maharishi, the Beatles' guru? One of them mantra'd, "Don't worry, be happy," which, no doubt surprisingly at this remove, attracted countless devotees. As they say, you had to be there. Recently, the writer tells Bob he remembers him enthusing back in the day that some spiritual teacher was celebrated by his acolytes for emitting only a single daily white pearl of bodily waste. Not exactly parting the Red Sea, the writer felt at the time. Bob, unfazed, responds mildly, "This is something you recall that I do not." But that single white pearl. Is writing not similar? Though one also expects to find the unprocessed, undigested. Under the eaves, if nowhere else.

Under the eaves. The writer is trying to put his house in order. But if he does that, what will remain? For people like him, or can it be for him only, might packing it up be synonymous with packing it in? During another 5 P.M. supper at Fat Apple's, Bob refers the writer to a verse of Buddha's teachings in *The Dhammapada*:

> I have passed in ignorance through a cycle of many rebirths, seeking the builder of the house. Continuous rebirth is a painful thing. But now, housebuilder, I have found you out. You will not build me a house again. All your rafters are broken, your ridgepole shattered. My mind is free from active thought, and has made an end of craving.

This from Bob, gifted builder of so many beautiful structures! And what a vision is Buddha's, urgent need to be liberated from the sorrow of an endless cycle of birth and death. Wisdom thus a destructive force, ending desire. Non-attachment. Tearing down one's house.

Writer pulling up in front of the garage. Early dark, nearly Thanksgiving, Venus pulsing in the west, Mars up over the hills. Through the first gate: magnolia in bloom, once again white blossoms arriving with the onset of winter. Go figure. Through the second gate—sliding the bar open, closed. To the left, jasmine draping, draping. And, dead ahead, aloes as usual having appropriated terrain while the writer was out. Sighing, he thinks he should negotiate with them before there's no lawn left. Colonizing, hyper-green, five feet in diameter, palm tree–like trunks, rosettes of rubbery, foot-long, ovate leaves, core shaft of new leaves ready to unfurl. The aloes have thrived on the writer's thirty-year watch, though he's neither cared for nor disturbed them. Proximities: adjacent to the cottage, the aloes know quite a bit about the writer. Have witnessed comings and goings, heard sounds of love, spleen. Might someday blackmail the writer, be called on to testify against him. Perhaps, he thinks, perhaps he should do more for them.

Vectors. As the writer has aged, the aloes have grown stronger, larger, more…virile. The writer's friend Jessica, self-described witch/herbalist/fortuneteller/wise "womb-in," as she puts it, asserts these aloes are all male.

"Then how have they replicated?"

"Self-propagating." Which, Jessica argues, means asexual reproduction, sperm and egg not fusing, plant budding off a miniature clone. Information leaving the writer to plumb the implications, his oh-so-familiar fate. As in, Do books contain the author's exact genetic material?

Now, on the doorstep in the dark—no porch light, better to keep the cottage hidden—the possibly or not-quite self-propagating writer fumbles with key. Mutters, "The dead of night." And then, as if conversing with someone—the eavesdropping aloes?—asks, "But who are the dead of night?" Who indeed.

Cottage: behind fences, through gates, tucked away. A hideout: "safe place for hiding (usually from the law)." Over the decades, the writer's gone to only one writer's colony, has preferred his own refuge (Latin, *fugere*, to flee—see fugitive, subterfuge). His shelter. Asylum! Inviolable, not to be despoiled. Secluded (with archaic meanings of secreting, confining). So, cottage as…sanctuary? Or, cottage as writer's retreat. Retreat, the writer reminds himself, not to be confused with rout. Agoraphobia, dread of being in an open space (from *agora*, ancient Greek, the marketplace): for all his travels, at times the writer has had to force himself out of the house.

"Away from home": in the early 1990s, the writer had a three-month traveling fellowship to the South Pacific: Fiji, Samoa, Rotuma, also sailing the Koro Sea, the Tasman Strait—to Yanutha, Thombia, Yavu, Raranitingga. On his return to northern California, the cottage was…opulent. Hot water! Washing machine! And the writer's possessions—books; this jacket, that vest—confirming parts of his life, self. Memory painted in object by object. Erotics of travel replaced by erotics of the domestic. Not to mention luxuriant privacy, after being strange among so many strangers. Countless responses to, say, his shaved head in the small lands of big hair. Home safe, a bit stunned, the writer unpacked a voyager's treasures, surveyed his domain. Felt like a buccaneer at long last coming up on safe harbor. Beaching and careening the hull of the self, caulking, scraping, laying in stores.

Here and gone. Systole, diastole. Ceronetti writes,

> The home fosters madness and nervous illnesses: *prison* and *dung heap*, in the words of the Buddhist. I love my home, but I am happy when I am far away. I do not see the bars, my reason is calm, my thoughts have freer reign, and my habits change. Those who have no home, who are born nomads, may never know mental illness.

Nomads. The writer thinks of wandering mendicants in India, parting from house and family to become holy indigents. The writer knew a fellow, maybe sixty-five, who left his wife and successful stores he'd established with the plan of living in his station wagon on the outskirts of towns in North Dakota and Wyoming. Or so the writer remembers the man explaining before he took off. The writer wonders how it all worked out.

So many returns to the cottage. From, say, the ranch in Bodega in the late '70s and early '80s. Almost always the one-hour drive at night, to see as little of the exurb as possible. Purist, fastidious in pickup truck. Or back from friends and book biz in New York City, again surprised appreciation for the quiet of this campus town.

Also, of course, returns from Boston. During the months of his mother's hospitalization in late 1983 and early 1984 there were many flights cross-country, back and forth, forth and back, until the writer became unable to discern which coast was the point of departure. He'd exiled himself from Boston much of the previous two decades, but retained a number of close ties, was an annual visitor. He'd arrive to do consulting work for his friend Neil's foundation, stay three or four weeks with his roommate from college, once more appraise the city he'd been raised in. But always he'd depart.

In California those post-sixties years, many people were belatedly planning to return not just to school and credentialing but to where they grew up. Abruptly, California was only where they'd gone to get free of family or hometown until strong enough to be themselves. Or perhaps time just had to pass, and California was where time could do that. In some cases, departing California was about limit, defeat: people couldn't make it without clan and childhood connections, either in their personal lives or in the world of work. Or maybe it was blood and water, blood being thicker than, and in the end California was water.

"Why don't you just go back where you came from?" One of the litany of childhood putdowns in Boston. But then again, in adulthood, fair question. The writer still had a plethora of connections there. And what made the possibility of return more real was available well-paying, interesting work. Commanding respect in the world of nonprofits and social service bureaucracies, Neil was in a position to open all kinds of doors. The writer was tempted. Though his father had died eleven years before, could his story not be a variant of the parable of the prodigal son? Return with reconciliation, celebration. The lost, now found. At this watershed moment—death of a second parent; turning forty—was it not time for homecoming? So many kinds of knowledge of that city were in him. The writer's classmates, grammar school through college. Layerings over years that make for richness, knowledge. The presence of the writer's older sister and her large family. The presence, after death, of the writers' parents in so many peoples' memories—his mother, phenomenally accomplished poet, actress, singer; his father, legendary physician.

There was also his parents' apartment: the writer and his siblings had yet to clear it, and he was living there as they readied their mother's memorial ceremony. He could just…stay on. Why not? Well, the writer again heard Joni Mitchell in *Blue* yearning for California, singing of a Paris "so old and cold and settled in its ways." It wasn't only that Boston was relentlessly hierarchical and constricted; it's that there the writer couldn't help being part of the problem. Felt, as he put it to himself, embourgeoisified. Didn't like the feeling. "To have a horror of the bourgeois is bourgeois," Jules Renard noted in his journal. Such a good line, inducing the writer to think Renard had it right.

Bob picked him up at San Francisco Airport. As they drove across the Bay Bridge, ships at anchor, sky blue, cloudless, the writer asked himself, "What am I returning to?" Chimera California! But at this moment, writer deracinated in so many ways, profoundly unhoused, now California appeared a white cube, modernist gallery. Here, having unsettled himself, the writer as artist would settle…down. Free—compelled!—to go on inventing himself, this space otherwise in so many aspects vacant. Vacant, that is, except for his narrative.

Back in the 1970s, meeting through their literary agent, Chester and the writer became friends. Writer in his early thirties, third book just out, Chester in his fifties, author of several novels. Recently divorced bachelor living in the country, soon to build a small house in the redwoods. All solar, lots of windows, fruit trees and garden, garlic beds/garlic shed, grape arbor, hummingbird squadron at the feeders, zooming, darting, hovering. And, despite the loft's double bed, the place designed for one. There would be women overnight, but as visitors. Chester's private domain. Brave, and stubborn, to be alone there in the country, rural days often achingly slow. And now, past eighty, Chester still writing, gracious host/wonderful cook/marvelous mythologizer. Still on his own. As, despite trepidations, he has chosen to be.

Chester's friend for thirty years—aging is when you start counting in decades—the writer reconsiders Chester's presence in his life. Such unsought reappraisals are increasingly frequent, inescapable: figures in one's saga change shape, position. *Harbinger:* forerunner, shadow of what's to come. Via Middle English and Old French, "person sent on to arrange lodging." Though savoring his own routines, the writer wouldn't say he resolved the cottage be just for one. There were years and years of the close and constant presence of another. But now, like Chester, he's a writer on his own.

Chester's beautiful house, also aging, in need of major repairs.

The writer's cottage. The writer remembers "The Three Little Pigs." Houses of straw, sticks, bricks. Blown down, or not.

Thinking about building materials, retracing footsteps, the writer goes back to his first fiction, thirty years before: when and how did he first make use of the cottage? Leafing through *Who Wrote the Book of Love?* the writer finds a story he'd forgotten but, starting the opening sentence, instantly remembers in detail: "He would have been hard pressed to precise what made him want to buy a house." A couple is making a bid on a small place tucked away in the hills, site of an old ranch, but the husband immediately suffers buyer's remorse. "Insurance, taxes, repairs, mortgage payments…he who for so long had needed no more than his health and a pack on his back. Home ownership felt like just the kind of puddle a man could drown in." As it turns out, a carpenter friend inspecting the place finds it riddled with problems—no more than a shack really. The couple withdraws its offer, husband nonetheless despondent: he'd already settled in, coveted the site's tranquil beauty.

Now, back looking at wildly overpriced houses in less appealing locations, the protagonist realizes that what he wants is beyond their means. Begins to look at his wife as if from a great distance, takes stock of her extraordinary virtues. But then, recalling the women he'd dated who would have the resources to help buy the house he desires, "he wished she had money, yes, he wished she had money. And, it occurred to him, since she had none he might be better off with someone who did."

Part of the writer's life: to wince rereading one's own work. Writer remembering his interest in taking a felt emotion and exploring where it might go. Hyperbolizing to create, get to the heart of, story.

Turning from the wide world to look hard at the domestic. Requiring a bit of sangfroid, decades ago, to write and, decades later, to read.

Chilled, the writer turns to the last story in *Who Wrote the Book of Love?* about a man far from home who imagines his wife: "He sees her lying in bed, morning sun brightening the room, three cats for a blanket; bicycling off to dance class, closing the gate behind her; mixing grains for breakfast cereal." In his hotel room, the man has a nightmare: there's a war going on; he has to make his way home on foot. At the moment the man wakes from the dream, drenched in sweat, he still has miles to go. Finally, business trip finished, at last the man achieves his destination:

> Once there, all he so recently only imagined quickly paints itself in. The plants, the rugs, his books, the bed, a quilt, the cats...Waking in the middle of the night, he walks restlessly around the house checking the doors. Seeing his wife in the bed, hair spread wide over the pillow, chin as always tilting up and away, he thinks, smiling to himself, that of course he who returns has never really left.

Sweet sentiment, and, rereading after so many years, the writer's relieved. Still, now curious, he takes down his second book of stories, tales of the "material plane." This was the world his characters were trapped in, but with the consoling—amusing?—intimation that there were other, better worlds. In *Who Wrote the Book of Love?* the writer had described a neighborhood:

> mostly small two-story houses or four-room cottages with attics. The building code—encouraging a large tax base—allows construction to within a foot of the property line; walls of adjoining homes are often only two

feet apart…Most of these structures are freestanding, but on warm weekends the cumulative effect is of a tenement that's been flattened and spread.

Nor was this a good season: because of drought,

water controls were being imposed, and the smog was heavier than ever. All neighborhood noises seemed amplified by the dirty air. Tempers were short, nights hot enough to justify homicide.

In his second book of stories, the writer again described that neighborhood:

The only hitch was that there were almost as many dogs as people…perhaps twenty-five dogs within a three hundred-foot radius [of the protagonist's home]. There had recently been a rash of robberies, and then a rapist had started to work the area. Even people who loathed dogs now kept one stationed in the yard.

In "Some Savage Present," the protagonist fights with recalcitrant neighbors about their barking dogs, contemplates dognapping. He seems to be living up to one of the book's epigraphs, Tinbergen on stickleback fish: "Alternating between the urge to attack and to escape, neither of which it can carry out, it is finally driven by its tension to find an outlet in an irrelevant action."

Three decades earlier, dreaming and shaping these stories, the writer encountered a roofer working on the place next door. Young, handsome, prep school–educated, and, he made clear, fallen aristocrat. The writer could relate: then in his early thirties, he'd improvised a life that included fellowships, consulting work, occasional semester as visiting writer, good reviews, interesting editing work. But he was asking something of the world it wasn't giving him, or something of himself he was having trouble carrying off. Like more than one of his characters, the writer seemed to believe there was a station to which he should be restored.

In another story, the narrator's in high dudgeon:

> I'm saying not only that this was no time for visionaries, but also that opportunists had run themselves ragged. Dreams hustled into so many marketable commodities you could get embarrassed for the species. And I kept hearing, all the time, from walking shards, about therapy for the whole being.

Continuing his rant, he describes his war with himself as he stops smoking:

> Phones rang incessantly in my pineal gland; I was a beached fish gasping in the sun. Snorting coke to suppress my nicotine craving (manifesting itself externally in budlike excrescences I ascertained to be yaws), I ran through a thousand bucks, quick, and contracted a mild case of megalomania. My irritation increased as I saw subordinate sections of my psyche assert their primacy. I seemed to be at school in myself, majoring in four-letter words, minoring in scatology. Though intermittently aware of what my language sounded like, I was only the more depressed, perhaps because even when nothing seemed particularly wrong, I had the sensation that the depression lever in my cerebellum had been permanently tripped. I was forever on the verge of tears.

The Verge of Tears. Could've been the narrator's honorific: "Ladies and Gentlemen, now introducing to you…" Unlike his characters, of course, the writer was fashioning story, career—being!—of such stresses. Seemed to be insisting that whatever his sense of displacement or dislocation, to stay in the cottage and make art was the solution. If, also, part of the problem. "Granted the cottage is straw," writer as spin-meister might have been arguing, "watch this: pure gold."

A neat conceit, better had the writer never read *Walden*. When the farmer "has got his house," Thoreau argued, it may be "the house that has got him…we are often imprisoned rather than housed in them and the bad neighborhood to be avoided is our own scurvy selves."

In *The Tango Lesson*, a writer/director, played by writer/director Sally Potter, has an affair with her tango teacher, is multi-partnered in a bravura session with three (male) teachers, and makes a movie-within-the-movie in which the tango teacher-lover is an actor she directs. Triumphalist dance dreams; student/teacher. When the writer learns basic salsa, besides his weekly group class he takes a biweekly private lesson. In her late twenties, his teacher Kristiaan allows slow acquisition of new moves, lots of repetitions, lest turns merge, dissolve. Salsa oblivion. A novice at partnered dance, the writer does know mentoring, respects Kristiaan's patience, humor. Realizes the self-as-student hates to fail the teacher. More than once, Kristiaan and the writer work on a turn he's making difficult. Brain, limbs, seizing, though in a day or two of practice back at the cottage it usually comes clear.

With Kristiaan, the writer is a dancer he'd not otherwise be. Their turns transpire as if in weightless slow motion; knowing where to go with such ease, she leaves him extra time, her grace wordlessly suggesting what he can aspire to. And of course she's "back-leading" him, though he is "the leader." The writer's reminded of surfing at dawn on "morning glass"—no wind, shape of the wave unblemished. Kristiaan is thus the first partner with whom he can really appraise what's passing between them. And what might that be? Well, at Kristiaan's apartment he's as usual permitting—goading—himself to move toward the heart of what's latent. Wanting to acknowledge whatever's being evoked by, say, Kristiaan's powerfully level gaze.

Kristiaan, teacher. Male/female in close contact. Resonances, ambiguities. Nurse? Masseuse? Kristiaan's attentiveness is centered, (disconcertingly?) neutral, (expressively?) expressionless, quietly expectant without suggestion of self-interest. Evokes a cat's self-containment, self-possession, but then, who knows what the cat's thinking? The writer's reaction to Kristiaan's gaze makes him think of what he's read about transference in Freudian therapy: patient—floundering, attempting to decipher inscrutably silent authority figure—reverts to childhood modes. Salsa regression? Kristiaan as the mother one loved, hated, who neglected you, loved someone else more, gave (what you hoped was) unconditional love? In fact, sessions at Kristiaan's apartment do remind the writer of childhood—of his cello teacher, peering down her bodice as she'd bend lovingly over the instrument cradled between her legs. The inaudible overtone of erotic curiosity.

One day Kristiaan offers a new turn. The follower steps away, leader advancing, his left hand placing her right, palm out, in the small of her back: three steps, pause. In the turn's second half, leader's *right* hand now on follower's right, he pulls her into a turn as if yanking the starter cord on a two-cycle engine. As if unraveling her.

The writer's much drawn to that putting of the follower's hand behind her back. Freezing the frame, he sees her elbow perforce bending as forearm and hand are tucked behind lower back. Breasts and genitalia exposed. While compliance of followers familiar with this turn is reflexively collaborative, those who haven't danced it are unprepared for such an opening of the self. May resist, elbow locking, confused by what's intended. If previously comfortable in the collaboration, a partner may ask the writer to do it again so she can deliver such (protected, theatrical) acquiescence. Or sometimes as they dance, the writer will describe the beginning of the turn just as they try it. "I'm going to place your right hand behind your back..."

Steps, missteps. The writer's never dated a student, even decades earlier as occasional visiting professor when colleagues and students seemed to consider such interchange part of the curriculum. Though avoiding bureaucracies and organizations, the writer needed the unalloyed *mana* of teaching every few years, both for itself and to connect in some modest way to his father's legacy of service. In the mid-1970s, when he first taught, a barefoot student in OshKosh B'Gosh coveralls would come to office hours each week, marvelously unencumbered breasts offered to his eyes as she'd lean over his desk. Writer thoughtfully concluding he should keep the door wedged open. And no doubt Kristiaan's fended off advances in clubs or class. But now, writer as student, what does he want from his teacher? Well, despite that amiable boyfriend emerging from Kristiaan's bedroom, the writer wants his teacher to...fall in love with him. Not because she's smitten with, say, his books, but because of his dazzling progress as dancer. This though he's making no such progress. And though, come to that, Kristiaan's just not his type.

Student/teacher. Two days a week, first steady job in his life, for the last ten years the writer hikes to campus and back. Twenty minutes going (uphill), fifteen minutes home to the cottage. Late January: in the front yard, lilies across from the aloe surging, unfurling (reminding him of the inexorable amaryllis in his mother's hospital room as she was dying). Out toward the street, plum and magnolia in blossom. Familiar northern California cycle of several days' downpour followed by high blue clearing. One afternoon, home after a late-morning class at Kristiaan's, storm clouds gathering, the writer tucks an umbrella under his arm and heads out the door for his office hours and three-hour seminar. Up Virginia past all the cherry trees in pink, right on Milvia, left on Francisco, down Shattuck, up Center, inhaling the rich fragrance of the redwood grove at the foot of campus, admiring the roiling creek.

Class. Still early in the semester, starting as usual with an invocation, communion. Circulating Xeroxes of an excerpt from J. A. Baker's *The Peregrine*, round the seminar room as each student, seriatim, reads a paragraph:

> Hawk-hunting sharpens vision. Pouring away behind the moving bird, the land flows out from the eye in deltas of piercing colour. The angled eye strikes through the surface dross as the obliqued axe cuts to the heart of a tree. A vivid sense of place grows like another limb.

J. A. Baker, then workshopping the day's two student stories. Shared insights, laughter, growing trust. Junk food, some of it purveyed by the writer—good for a sense of shared purpose—being munched. Writer surveying the class, thinking a Chaucer could narrate the semester's pilgrimage, tales.

Six thirty. Class done, the writer walks down three flights with several students. "Anyone going north?" he asks as they approach the Free Speech Movement Cafe. The air's warm, incredibly moist. Tropical, suddenly.

Janice, a Chinese-American, nods. Reserved, pensive, but occasionally smiling appreciatively to herself. At a line in a poem they read aloud or another student's comment. As if confirmed she made the right choice in loving literature, being in this classroom. An English major, she wants to do editing and to write, get an MFA.

As the writer and Janice head down toward the foot of campus, suddenly it begins to rain. Hard. Very hard. Both of them laughing at being so abruptly exposed to the elements, the writer presses the button on his small black umbrella, offers the crook of his arm. Already drenched, they're walking very fast. The writer's shoes and jeans are waterlogged; Janice's white blouse is soaked, erect nipples against wet cotton.

Arm-in-arm under the small umbrella, they continue to race against, what, getting caught in the rain? Rivers and pools of water in the street, sewers backed up. Up Oxford, down Hearst, up Shattuck, down Francisco, right on Milvia. Left on Virginia. Two blocks from the writer's cottage.

Perhaps it's the lesson with Kristiaan, sexual ambiguities so vivid, or power of the storm, or Janice's arm in his—touching a student, being touched—or that they're talking about being chilled, but now the writer is thinking "Singing in the Rain." Or that he should offer Janice tea at the cottage. A hot bath. Bathrobe. Scotch and almonds. They're still moving very fast. Cantering, he thinks.

"Stop!" Janice exclaims. "We're here." Small 1950s apartment building, grotty: student housing. They stand just inside the open garage.

"Well, thank you for the umbrella," she says, dropping his arm, and they both laugh, look each other over.

"As your professor," the writer says, reminding them who they are, "I have to tell you you're all wet." Janice smiles, that private smile of savor. Says nothing. "See you next week," the writer adds.

When they leave the shelter of the garage, Janice turns, waves, runs for the staircase. Rain pelting the umbrella, the writer strides down the street several hundred yards, then is through one gate, the other, at the door of the cottage. Inside.

Kicking off his shoes, dropping his wet clothes on the hallway Mexican tile Bob thought of, installed, the writer runs a bath. Pours—himself—a scotch.

Wallace Stevens: "The house was quiet and the world was calm." Once more, toward midnight, writer alone with a book, under the welcome weight of five blankets. Reading Bob Dylan's memoir. Comic, almost, Dylan's refusal to acknowledge the simplest truths, his persistent opposition to the obvious. That he's Jewish, or how ruthless a young man he was. Nonetheless, Dylan offers a rich portrait of an artist in the self-making. As a kind of Cuisinart, ingesting or appropriating traditional folk songs, Woody Guthrie's neo-authentic compositions, Brecht/Weil, performance art, Rimbaud, Van Ronk's version of "House of the Rising Sun" (but no mention of the role of drugs in the [re]configuring of his imagination). And then the spewing out of songs channeling, defining the country's collective unconscious. Followed by, apparently, years of the loss of his gift.

Midnight. Finishing the Dylan, thinking of his own untellables, the writer returns to Adam Phillips on Houdini. As before, he's struck by Phillips himself as magician, such deft insights, inversions. Phillips seemingly more forthcoming than Dylan, though Dylan might observe Phillips only appears to have less to protect. ("I didn't want to give away anything that was dear to me," Dylan says in the film *No Direction Home*.) Here, in any case, speaking of escape and escape artists, Phillips quotes a Hungarian proverb: "It is better to fear than to be frightened."

Intrigued but exhausted, the writer puts NB in the margin. Will return. Pushing along, now not only in, but, as they say, ready for, bed, the writer comes to this: "The absence of desire and real death, of which the death of desire is a foreshadowing, are the two great hauntings."

One in the morning. Turning out the light, the writer tries to grapple with *hauntings*. Then, in the darkness's loud silence, he's overtaken not by final disintegration but by a moment of contentment. Smiling, thinks of the word *bliss* (check *blithe,* he tells himself). Feeling that in the diction and insights of these and other narratives he's doing his true work, has stopped running (away). Has found a—demanding—peace. Eyes closed, snug under the five blankets, the writer tells himself he should get up, go to the dictionary for the roots of *evade, escape, avoid.* Of *hide, seek...*

"Afraid. Of, for instance, being alone with a book." One of the writer's epigrams. True as true can be. But just not tonight.

Nineteen eighty-three, moment still being processed by the writer. Successful fashion photographer from NYC, in San Francisco for a shoot, comes to the cottage. They've known about each for years: baby sister of an old friend. As they talk in the living room, day waning, she describes her wonderful two-year-old son, almost in the same breath tells the writer she slept only one time with her son's father, whom she has yet to inform because then he'll demand parental rights, that she has not slept with anyone since. Lots of information quickly presented; the writer marvels. Concludes: strike three. His friend will be angry, a mix of attraction and censuring between siblings there; and she clearly…has some problems. This noted, he sees himself offer his hand, and they go into the bedroom. Lie down, embrace. Kiss. Kiss some more. She starts to cry, sob. Strike four, the writer thinks, fingering the top button of her blouse. Crane flies watching, waiting for what comes next.

About the writer's industrial ear protectors: two pairs in the study, one upstairs, one in the bedroom, five unopened packages in the garage. Two sets when he travels. The writer's use of—dependence on—these "ear-muffs," as one manufacturer puts it, dates back to when he lived with Katrin, a kind of victory, being barely able to hear the neighbors' barking dogs. Or, in a New York City hotel, to blot out honking horns. Early on, the writer proselytized for the ear protectors, though his friends' first question was usually a disbelieving, "You sleep with them on?" He did. Does. Often reads with them on. Generally writes with them on, long since habituated to a certain quality of silence (unless there's Afro-Cuban music on the stereo).

Some lovers have found the headphones—and nightcap for his shaved head—understandable, have their own nocturnal prostheses: light mask; bite guard for teeth grinding; sleeping pill. But several women have resisted the apparent finality of the moment before slumber when the writer reaches for the ear protectors. One deft lover would immediately place a leg over the writers' calves before lifting an ear piece to whisper, "I love you." Then gently repositioning it.

Morning, alone or not, writer waking. Rolling to the edge of the bed. Sitting up. Standing. Catching sight of himself, naked except for headphones, in the wall mirror. Thinking, *Ludicrous*. Taking off the ear protectors, placing them on the handle of the study door.

A day in the life. This particular dawn, as he has before, the writer wakes muttering, "Help me," though he has no notion of to whom he's speaking. Nor any sense someone will. Feels, thinking it over, that he's put himself beyond help. Or, perhaps, that whatever's besetting him, we are all beyond help. Bare feet on cold wood floor, the writer wonders where he goes during sleep. To some Night School or Office of Accounting, perhaps.

Out of bed, naked. "'Denuded,'" he mutters, could just be "'nuded.'" Dressing in the dark—black Calvin Klein briefs, black Armani Exchange tee shirt, black cotton pants, black sandals. Struggling to remember coffee mug/car keys/door key, grunting with one ache or another, the writer lumbers out to the front gate. Bends for Home Delivery of the *New York Times* and *San Francisco Chronicle* at the front gate. Stands, looks around. Venus enormous, low in the east. And, to the right, not, as it seemed, a large cat but a raccoon. There on the sidewalk, masked, staring, brazen, giving no ground.

"Don't shoot," the writer says to the raccoon. "I'm going."

Into the car to drive the few blocks to his local café. Yes: out of the cottage. Imperative, he long ago came to believe, to each day make himself enter the wide world. Song of the self-employed.

Coffee shop, 6:15 A.M. Elephant graveyard: only a few old(er) men. And the Guadalajara-born baristas.

"Donde estan las mujeres?" the writer asks José, and they both laugh. Never any women at this hour.

While José makes the writer's double cappuccino, Bob arrives, on his way to feed the feral cats at his shop before heading to the job site.

"You're up early," Bob says.

"Don't confuse it with virtue. I had to get out of bed to write something down. Seemed important."

"Let's hear it. "

"'There's no more going forward, only going back.' It sounded better before I was fully awake."

"How about, 'There is no forward, there is no back'?" And then, a smile over his shoulder, Bob's off to the cats.

Taking his mug, the writer sits down, leafs through the papers. Checks TV listings in the *Sporting Green*. Ah, Red Sox game on ESPN. Roots.

Quick drive home. Afro-Cuban music on the stereo, a ballad from Issac Delgado's *Prohibido* warranting a few moves of air salsa in the living room. Over to the kitchen table for an infusion of hummus/whole grain crackers/apple. Tapping the day's correctives out of the pill box. And then to the computer. Back into the manuscript—this manuscript. Yet another draft printed out, simulacrum of book text. After the will-driven bulldozing of early versions, the more tranquil pleasures of slow progress, deepening. This despite the perennial underlying anxiety of wondering if the entire enterprise is somehow misguided: who, after all, set it all in motion? Revising, in any case, expanding, paring. And again. Text becoming richer than the writer had imagined. Moving toward the condition in which, as Sallustius might have said of literary nonfiction, "Of course these things never happened quite this way, but are always."

Writer building the text; building the self who writes/who wrote. You can immerse yourself in books, read them, create them, but it's not possible to live in them all the time. To be them. Which can occasion dismay, feeling of dislocation. One solution is to keep books close at hand. On the shelves of the cottage's downstairs bedroom are books waiting to be speed-read or savored, a few to be kept in the library in the garage, some traded for scrip at Moe's Books. But, for years, in the cottage on the shelf there is Philip Larkin's *Collected Poems,* reviews and clippings about the author stuffed inside. Though the writer admires several Larkin poems, he sets his star by just one—"The Old Fools." "It's only oblivion, true," Larkin writes of after-death, again making the writer laugh. And of people the old dimly remember, "each looms/Like a deep loss restored." *A deep loss restored.* Not to mention the image of the old "crouching below/Extinction's alp…never perceiving how near it is."

Larkin the man? No role model. John Updike, not afraid to champion his betters, acknowledges Larkin's "caustic shyness" and the "dislikable crustiness" in Larkin's letters—Updike might have cited locker room misogyny, racial hatreds, and rage—while arguing for the "generous, deep-breathing self-transcendence" of Larkin's best poems. There's humor in Andrew Motion, Larkin's biographer (later, England's poet laureate, obliged to versify the marriage of Charles and Camilla), imagining himself Larkin's moral superior. Larkin: self-confessed masturbator & collector of pornography but, deplorably, isolato seeing three women at once just before he died. Of course we believe Motion could never do such things. But as Martin Amis writes of Motion and others on Larkin, "They think they judge him? No. He judges…their hedging and trimming."

Hedging, trimming. What's in a word? Recently, the writer's in the living room reading a journal essay about a dissident author, bumps into "delicious" in the reviewer's characterization of a book of poems. Delicious. OK, the writer thinks, the reviewer's "recuperating" a word, as they say in academia (*recuperate* itself recuperated from post-op hell a decade or so ago), though this minor ambition upstages the object of his inquiry. And is the reviewer not trying to elicit the reader's consent to this use of the word? To insist the reviewer's winning enough to win the reader over? The reviewer himself: delicious? Or...*meretricious* ("alluring by false attractions," from Latin, of prostitutes).

The cottage. Another day. Getting late. The writer puts down the review, takes out his Larkin, wants the last words before sleep to remind him what he hopes for from language. Often, his fiction seminar students are deferential to poems, as if poetry's ipso facto beyond them.

"Don't be afraid," the writer had told his class that week. "Poems are frequently just weak prose that couldn't go the distance. As Ezra Pound said, poetry should be at least as well written as prose."

The students had looked disbelieving: poets are skilled propagandists. Then the writer had passed out Xeroxes of "The Old Fools" for several of them to read aloud, seriatim.

"This is so," the writer added, Xeroxes circling the room, "except for poems that make you wish you could live by and in such language. Which you can't, quite."

Looking for inspiration, the writer's rereading *Let Us Now Praise Famous Men,* James Agee's obsessively detailed incantation about the lives of impoverished sharecroppers in Depression Alabama. Of a "lighted coal-oil lamp," for instance:

> The glass was poured into a mold, I guess, that made the base and bowl, which are in one piece; the glass is thick and clean, with icy lights in it. The base is a simply fluted, hollow skirt; stands on the table; is solidified in a narrowing, a round inch of pure thick glass, then hollows again, a globe about half flattened, the globe-glass thick, too; and this holds oil, whose silver line I see, a little less than half down the globe, its level a very little—for the base is not quite true—tilted against the axis of the base.
>
> This "oil" is not at all oleaginous, but thin, brittle, rusty feeling, and sharp; taken and rubbed between forefinger and thumb, it so cleanses their grain that it sharpens their mutual touch to a new coin edge, or the russet nipple of a breast erected in cold; and the odor is clean, cheerful, and humble.

Eager to dignify these people, to be the one to dignify them, Agee was perhaps unaware that any torrent of words could leave a reader hearing all an author wouldn't say. Still, smitten by the book as a young man, now again placing himself under Agee's influence, the writer takes another look around the cottage. Rediscovers the large kitchen window. What to do with it? He counts its panes. Twelve.

Twelve. A closet transcendentalist, the writer waits to locate the heroic in the present moment.

The window. In the later 1980s, then past age forty, the writer sat at the kitchen table having supper with Serena, with whom he was, as it happened, to spend more than a decade. He'd made garlic linguine with lots of garlic, his one dish, had a bowl of fresh-grated Romano. Plate of raw red cabbage, raw carrots, celery, endive. *Crudités* implying he might have cooked them. Enjoying the meal, Serena generously pretended to believe there were other *spécialités* of this bachelor's *maison*.

As they were eating, an apparition manifested itself in the window. A visage, deciphered: Betti's. The writer had slept with Betti, once, and she was (not unreasonably?) insistent in phone calls that so doing obligated him to see her again. Thwarted, she'd shown up uninvited. Which might have been the end of the windowpanes, except that Betti's visit unsettled Serena. Until recently, for five years after separating from Katrin the writer had dated so much and so many that he'd become unable to remember to whom he'd told what. So now, with Serena, this remarkable woman—strikingly beautiful but not knowing it, of great integrity, hardworking, modest, and locked in a custody struggle with an abusive former spouse—now the writer happily chose monogamy. But...the phone kept ringing when Serena stayed the night, answering machine assiduously clicking and grinding, recording messages she couldn't hear, calls from one former lover or another making her anxious. Jealous. Angry. After a while, the writer wearied of placating. He'd decided to be with Serena only. Was that not enough? Enjoying friendships with other women was no crime, or so he argued, standing on Principle, which he might have admitted could be a self-serving perch over the great gulf of Error. In this period he got an answering service with a different number to which he could have calls forwarded, but by then, well, damage had been done.

What, really, was at stake for him in this? A lack of belief in conventional relationships, gestures? Hedging his bets? Refusing to promise more than he would deliver? Truly not wanting to devalue friendships by subjecting them to scrutiny? As for the twelve windowpanes in one large window, twenty years later the writer studies them. Three rows across, four in a row. Soon after the night Betti materialized out of the darkness, Serena—problem solver with mechanical aptitude and toolbox—installed blinds on the downstairs windows.

The writer and Serena, a subsequent moment. They'd been seeing each other several years. No question they loved each other, but the writer didn't want to get a larger place, share a household. This confounded Serena, drove her, finally, to something approaching resignation. Things one does not write. Should have written. Serena wanted help with a Personals Ad, to meet someone else. The writer was good with words, wasn't he?

"You'll never leave the cottage," Serena once said. The writer remembers thinking she was quite mistaken. Remembers, with a twinge, Serena in the doorway of her own home, yet again watching him depart. How much time he spent there, for years making the fifteen- or twenty-minute drive three or four days a week to help her son with his homework, savor another fine meal she prepared as if effortlessly, watch a video, but still often felt…remote. The town: upwardly mobile families who'd moved in for the very good public schools, also a layer of the upper-upper middle class. The place sobered the writer in ways he couldn't quite name. Echoed, perhaps, all he'd wanted to leave behind in Boston—strictured, cloying pleasures, joylessness? Never articulating it to himself, he never articulated it to Serena.

"Non, je ne suis jamais seul, avec ma solitude." Never alone, with my solitude. From a Georges Moustaki song Serena had loved since student days in France. Solitude *"fidèle comme une ombre."* Faithful as a shadow.

In the cottage's front yard, jasmine Serena planted engulfs one of the fences.

*S*ooner or later. *What day, what year? Making up for lost time.* Each a phrase the writer, not quite at a loss for words, wakes saying to himself at dawn one morning or another. Blearily repeats, so as not to forget. Shuffles into the study to write down, apparently believing shards of dreamtime hold special meaning. Still, he knows transmissions from the beyond are hardly unerring. "Death trap." Writer thinking of Boston's Coconut Grove nightclub fire when he was a child. Death trap?

"Nope," he tells himself as he sets down the syllables. "Death trip, fire trap."

Morning rituals. Opening the blinds on the twelve downstairs windows. "Blind leading the blinds," he tells himself. Writer in a bad mood. Internal monologue? Internal dialogue. A kind of parlando, he thinks, as if he's lost his true voice, speaking life's lyrics when he should be singing them.

"Pick a word, any word," he dares himself.

"All right, mo'fo'. *Squalid.* As in foul, repulsive, wretched, degraded. So to speak."

The writer grins. "Give me a moment." Then runs the table a la Jackie Gleason as Minnesota Fats. *"Squid, squab, squeamish, squall."* He pauses for effect. *"Squander. Squat. Squaw. Squeak. Squirrel. Squeeeeeeal."*

"Nice."

"Grudging, but thank you." He raises his eyebrows. "So, what's the question?"

"You thought of it too—it's about the *s-q-u*'s, as in skwolid."

"You mean, 'What happened to the *w*'s?' Like, why does *ph=f* in phone, *wh=h* in whore? You think questions about orthography will make *sqwalor* with a *w* less squalid?"

"*S-k-w-u,*" the writer replies. Spelling it out, cheered enough to head to the café for coffee and a skimming of the *New York Times.*

Back in the cottage, the writer checks the night's upwelling of email, cyberspace corollary of nocturnal ocean migration, masses of deep-sea fish, shrimp, and squid moving toward the surface to feed on plankton. Hunters, hunted: Message from Accounts Department. In the guise of eBay security, hustler trolling for account data. Or, lottery the writer didn't enter announces he's won. Another mail— Size Matters—offers Viagra. "Your money back without question ask (sic)."

There are also sagas of illness/jeopardy/political turmoil/treasure/death-bed illumination/lost next-of-kin. Proposed larceny. From, it says, Mrs. Jewel Taylor, estranged wife "to" the former president of Liberia, recently deposed. "My dear, With all sincerity and humility it is with deep pains I write you this message of wishful assistance to my predicament." Mr. Micawber thus invoked, to better "the lives of i and my children" the sender speaks of "$20m (Twenty Million United States Dollars)." The obligatory safety deposit box, "deposit certificate." Prospective "beneficiary to the funds," the writer is to "keep this project close to your heart," answer with phone number.

On the heels of which, lowercased kenneth yusuf, "Branch manager of Inter Continental Bank" in Lagos, has both story and proposition—"the intended business is thus." Foreigner died in Nigeria, had US$10.5 million in the bank, no next of kin. Now kenneth and his two colleagues at the bank want "you (being a foreigner) to be fronted as one of his next of kin." Writer's to forward his account and other "relevant documents"; it'll take "five working days to get the fund retrieved successfully without trace even now or in future." Kenneth offers 30% of the total "while 65% would be for i and my colleagues and the remaining 5% would be for any form of expenses." As they say, whatever.

Another mail anticipates the recipient's inevitable "Why me?":

> Concerning the reason why I choosed you, I will like to tell you how it happened. I do not know who I was going to appoint as my guardian. Now the time is running and I am getting more confused. I started asking God for directives on that. One day, I decided I was going to look for people contacts and profile and select any one that my mind told me to pick. I went to an internet center here in Abidjan Cote d'Ivoire were I present live and started searching…I got a lot of contact but I copied only three and took it home…I kept the names and was praying on it so that God will direct me…I trust you but I trust God the more because he will never fail me nor leave me.

Which mail is followed by one from Kenya. Similar setup: address/phone number needed "as i will instruct the officer in charge to deliver the consignment to you in your place on my behalf if only you are not going to betray us at the end." *If only you are not going to betray us at the end.* Oops, storyteller overreached: Freudian slip. The writer enjoys these cons, story with appeal to greed, presumption of gullibility. With verisimilitude: God *is* in the details. Here, since only the crazily avaricious could succumb, the writer's free to admire the bald-faced lie. And can these authors really care only about result, or is it the sheer exhilaration of telling such stories? "Dear Swiss Lottery Winner—watch out for unwarranted abuse of this program by some unscrupulous elements. To file for your claim please contact our trusted agent."

Trusted agents: recalling Melville's *The Confidence Man,* unbearably bleak vision of nineteenth-century America, the writer thinks of Vice President Cheney's side-of-the-mouth storytelling. Embarrassing: stagily manly, contrivedly forthright, this with unblinking head-tilted appraisal of the interviewer's credulity, sycophancy. Cheney's inside-the-Beltway verbal tic of "quite frankly," conveying that nothing, absolutely nothing he says will be straightforward.

Language used "to keep thought at bay," as Pinter put it, is not just for captors. Ibn al-Shaykh al-Libi, alleged al-Qaeda leader experiencing "rendition," that euphemism, to Egypt, confesses al-Qaeda members received chemical-weapons training in Iraq—testimony then used by Cheney to make the case for the impending Iraq war. Later, however, al-Libi recants, says he was tortured. Cheney and Ibn al-Shaykh al-Libi: narrative artists sharing the same palette.

Saturday night. Liv and the writer going dancing. Liv's twenty-six, MBA in international finance. Strong-willed, self-absorbed, avidly pursuing salsa. Reminding the writer of his own obsessiveness when he began. He's mentoring—they met at a local ballroom—but soon will have taught Liv all he knows.

Coming in to the cottage for the first time, she takes a look around, asks to use "the restroom." Well, the writer reminds himself, "bathroom" is also a euphemism, restroom no worse than toilet twice removed. And better than "the shitter," term of choice for young males in Boston in the 1950s.

Emerging, Liv asks, "Is there another restroom in the house?" The writer shakes his head. "But," Liv continues, "where's the shower?" The word *consternation* occurs to the writer, makes him smile.

No shower. Katrin loved baths. In his first novel, a young wife spends hours at a time in the bath, dozing, humming, sponging. Water dripping from the tap, mirrors clouded over, ceiling sweating. Candles flickering, her chin floating on the soapy water. Two decades later, in the writer's second novel, there's a young woman in the tub as her writer/lover enters the bathroom, Polaroid in hand. She faces the camera, one breast showing, the other obscured by a dictionary (!) that rests on the rim of the tub. Pubic hair visible just under the surface.

Art, life: the women who've spent the most time in the cottage have liked baths. A precondition, or are they self-selecting? More than once—every five or six years—Bob's taken a look at the bathroom, explained how much trouble it would be to install a shower. Recently, they discussed an outdoor redwood enclosure with shower in the front yard, though Bob is more interested in getting the writer to replace the aging living-room floor heater. Risk of carbon monoxide poisoning, Bob says, recommending a gas-fed, fuel-efficient, simulated log fire that could be installed in the fireplace.

Though Liv's inspecting the cottage as the writer gathers his things, she shows no interest in the writer's books. Doesn't much care that he's a writer one way or the other. Dancing is what she wants. And, maybe, "hooking up" when they return from San Francisco. He tries to imagine what it will be like, given her matter-of-factness. She plans on marriage—by thirty—and kids—two. Has this "game plan" but has not mentioned the word *love*.

"Ready?" Liv asks. She's driving, is eager to get moving.

The writer grabs his coat. As they head out the door, he feels protective of the cottage. Thinks, *Love my tub, love me.*

How people see the cottage. Scottish teenager, raised in a castle, deemed it a "bit empty." Japanese woman working in New York City walked in, exclaimed, "Minimalist!" Andrea, having read *The Beholder* before her first visit: "Looks like I thought it would." Mark, former student, laughed: "the factory!" Uli, professor of Victorian literature, exclaims, "Just what I've always wanted, though mine would be a mess, full of papers and books." And Binta, young artist-in-the-making, who sees how the cottage empowers. "Emptied of the unnecessary…Honed to the essentials of living—rest, repast, rejuvenation, and in the writer's case, reading…shelves periodically emptied and then refilled, books gleaned in preparation for a current project."

In fact, Binta may like the cottage more unambiguously than the writer. Occasionally, back from a gathering at someone's large house in the hills, he tastes relative deprivation. Once sat in the library of a beautiful old home, all fine woods and leather chairs—charms of the upper middle class—thinking that, unlike the owner, he would actually produce books in such a space. But then the writer will remember the cottage has been the intersection of several imperatives. Disposable income spent not on housing but, profligately, on time to write.

The writer's neighbors, husband and wife long married and devoted to each other, sought to live "mindfully," follow the spiritual path. "Healing" an ongoing aspiration, they decided on a "sage cleansing" of their home, Native American practice said to use the herb to integrate mind and body with spirit. For this elimination of the negative, they set down many little candles in a room upstairs. Somehow a fire got started. Lots of damage, a real mess. Several years later, house repaired, they divorced.

The writer wonders, *What's the moral?* Did the sage in fact produce domestic ablution? When you ask for purification, are you expecting something like your cleaning person's weekly visit, like "colonic irrigation," appointment with your dental hygienist? Perhaps the terms of this couple's contract with the sage should have been made explicit.

Despite so ambiguous an example, the writer tries to envision what it would take to cleanse the cottage, this though visitors always says how neat it is. He thinks of purification rituals in Boston when he was a child. Dirty words? Mouth washed out with soap, ceremony with a nice touch of the spiritual made literal. But as for cleansing the cottage? Nothing less than a conflagration, the writer concludes: small place, big fire.

Conflagrations. Leafing through the *Lotus Sutra*, interest spurred by Bob's quote from *The Dhammapada*, the writer finds the Buddha offering his disciples a parable. There's a huge house, decaying and rotting: "beams and ridgepoles are toppling dangerously." Fire breaks out, the father trying to lure his children to come out, though they are happily at play inside, don't even know what is meant by the word *fire*. We humans, of course, are children in the house of the self, suffering (fires of) birth, old age, sickness, death, grief, misery, stupidity, et cetera. Playing happily nonetheless.

The Buddha then retells the parable, house this time containing all kinds of evil creatures and places "stinking of excrement and urine,/Oozing with filth." Also ghosts "With heads like oxen,/Now eating human flesh,/And then devouring dogs," not to mention centipedes, millipedes, poisonous snakes, vipers. This litany of the horrors of the burning house goes on and on, and so the Buddha's argument about the cost of attachment and "greed/To all the defiling desires."

Hank Williams, you sang my life! The three plagues— flu/flies/rats—of the writer's humble cottage so graphically evoked, he laughs, checks his vital signs. Ready for a conversion experience? But sometimes even higher beings —or those telling stories in their name—don't know when to rest a case. After this second telling of the parable, the Buddha excoriates anyone who "slanders" the Sutra, promising eons in which they'll become dogs "repulsive to others," suffering hunger and thirst. Or, "They may become camels/Or they may be born among asses,/Always carrying heavy burdens/And beaten with sticks and whips,/Thinking only of water and grass." Or, as humans, they'll "be deaf, blind, and dumb,/Poor and decrepit… Swollen with water, or else dehydrated,/With scabs and boils…Their bodies will always stink/Of filth and impurity."

What a disappointment, the writer thinks. Truth is, he's never much liked being threatened about his response to story, even though he's of course imagined settling scores for the occasional hostile review. You know, encounter critic at party years later/impugn (wo)manhood/empty punch bowl over head, that kind of thing. So the writer tries to empathize with the Buddha or his disciple-scribes. Perhaps it was just this one (decaying) sutra—jeez, no prose is perfect. Or perhaps for all writers, whatever their cause, there's something about the prospect of being disregarded that just burns the…hell out of them.

Paladin, from the Latin, "officer of the palace," someone with royal privileges. Writer upstairs in the cottage, in the closet leafing through black dress shirts on hangers, picking one with textured pattern indented, raised. Embossed! Choosing a pair of black slacks. Removing shoe trees from a pair of black leather half-boots. Black knight into black night.

San Francisco, Mission District, Thursday night at ten. Unable to find a parking space, the writer pulls into a garage, leaves cell phone and house keys in the car. Traveling light for salsa. Something crosses his mind as he strides onto the street, but his attention is on what's ahead: Elbo Room, small club with superb local Cuban band. Several hours later, danced out, band having led the stampede, dancers stalking and braving the beat, the writer returns to the garage to find several disconsolate people in front of a locked gate. Closed at midnight, this in a neighborhood with lots of after-hours spots. What had earlier crossed his mind: five years before, the same thing had happened in North Beach.

Just then a cab pulls up, passengers disembarking. Providential. As the writer clambers in, the driver holds up his hand.

"Sorry, but I'll only take you across the bridge if I can smoke."

"I love secondhand smoke," the writer replies. And does, explaining that he used to be very good at Marlboros. To which the driver responds with the offer of a flat rate. Compatriots. Ah, well: the writer will have to **BART** over to San Francisco in the morning to pick up the car—a hassle, but not life threatening. Glass? Half full.

Twenty-five minutes later, once more at the cottage, paladin lifting up the rock for the extra set of keys. Writer as planner; everything in its place. Unlocking the lower lock, inserting the other key in the upper lock and…bolt doesn't turn. Won't turn.

How get into the cottage? The carpenter doing a small repair has left his extension ladder, which the writer lugs around to the back, mounts. Surveying the sloping attic roof below the open second-story window, he realizes he just can't make it. Will fall. Descending, he puts the ladder down. Tries the bathroom window, which is as usual open four inches, but the metal block *he's* placed inside precludes it from lifting higher. Coming around to the front of the cottage, the writer takes the smaller step ladder left by the carpenter, studies the downstairs bedroom window. Also open four inches, also with window block, but the writer thinks he can perhaps shake this window past it.

No. Nope. Two in the morning. Very, very tired. Salsa high long since evaporated. What to do? Having realized years ago that for all the protection it offers the cottage is of course permeable—what fortress is not?—the writer has thought to make it difficult to break in without actually breaking something. Now he weighs what to sacrifice, how many dollars it will cost. Still on the step ladder in front of the bedroom window, summoning up his karate training's focus, he makes a decision, with the heels of both hands strikes the sides of the frame one sharp blow. *SHAZAM:* the window leaps out of the frame and lands…on the bed. Not cracked, not broken. Something the repairman can reinstall come morning.

The writer climbs in. Turns on lights. Runs a bath. Embossed black shirt dropped by the front door to take to the cleaners. Shoe trees inserted. Apple from fridge. Home again.

Where did it all begin? One moment, the writer was in Hawai'i, rising and falling on the gentle swell, yet another time sitting up on his surfboard staring at Diamond Head at dawn. Part of his self-appointed task of figuring out how to write about water and light, which also had him reading anything that promised to help him find the words. From which came two (warm) ocean books, many months of travels in the South Pacific, and two collaborations with marine photographer Wayne Levin. A ten-year prose immersion. But as the writer was working to finish his second water book, a new project pressed at him, writer only just able to defer it.

The female nude. Did the idea come on a beach in Honolulu, as he laughed at his inability to decipher the Chinese character tattooed in the small of a young woman's back while wondering if she could? Was it the 1980s argument by some feminists that pornography was rape, writer reading such rhetoric as doing violence to complex truths? Or was it his biological clock, something about middle aging? For whatever reason, suddenly the writer was wading through art history and feminist discourse about the nude. And then, back home, as if inevitably putting an ad in a local paper. Figure models. Not to sketch or paint, but for portraits in words. His epiphany: Why should photographers and painters have all the fun? Had any writer ever done such a thing? Oh, he was elated, knew a book would come of it (as it did, though not the work of nonfiction he'd imagined).

The ad: ensuing flood of calls, a number of women calling again and again. One woman told him her therapist insisted she respond. Astonished, nonetheless the writer found something familiar in it: each commitment to write a book had begun with a sense of transgression, if only the carving out of time and space from an unwilling world. Prometheus a thief, the old tale tells.

The first model was a Filipina in her early thirties—a manicurist, she said. The writer had brought one of the chairs from the living room into the study, draped a (clean) towel over it. At his suggestion, the model undressed in the bathroom; walked in wearing pumps and sat down. The writer was at his desk computer, perhaps four feet from her pumps. As they say, he knew not what he was doing. Still, while he and the model chatted—when did she emigrate, what kind of place did she grow up in?—he began to type, decided his task was to describe face, breasts, pubic mound, looking hard while listening to her description of struggles with coworkers and customers. Watching her take in the study with all its books. As he typed, she said, admiringly, "You're a real intellectual." Writer at work.

She was standing when she said this, the writer's own admiring centered on her nipples in profile. But suddenly he was tired, suggested a break. At her request, he showed her the stack of books of paintings and photographs on his desk. They stood side by side, nearly joined at the hip, the writer thought, leafing pages of Manuel Bravo images as she praised one nude, was unimpressed by another. Looking at the photos in terms of the women's beauty, it seemed—whom she would desire to be, desire. When he then told her the session was more or less done, she responded, "So soon?"

"OK," he replied, "please sit down again." Back to work.

"When I used to model for a photographer," she suddenly said, "he always wanted me to show pink." Writer just beginning to process the word when she used both hands to open—no, spread wide—her labia.

Manners. When the writer was a child, on the rare occasion they had guests for dinner, the children were expected to rise as, making her entrance, their mother came down the stairs, swept into the music room. Also, the boys were to open car doors for women; and the male walked, always, nearer the curb.

The model's labia. "Thank you for showing me," the writer said. "That's very beautiful." Wondered if he should have used the plural. Wondered how long her hands were going to hold that pose. And then, a living and breathing update of Dürer's bulging-eyed *Draftsman Drawing a Nude,* resumed his typing.

The writer's legerdemain and, over the years, what of it insistently summons itself to the writer's mind. Conjuring his dive trip with marine photographer Wayne Levin to Costa Rica's Cocos Island, he'd tried to evoke both the extraordinarily fecund, unsettling marine life—everything predator or prey—and, determined to be thorough, the island's human history. Researching those hunting for pirate treasure, the writer described a seeker who spent twenty years on Cocos:

> A Portuguese shipmate let Gissler copy a map said to belong to a man who'd sailed with Benito Bonito; and years later, in Hawai'i, Gissler saw an old beachcomber's chart. Cocos again. Which led Gissler eventually to Boston to a son-in-law of Keating-the-Canadian...and to years digging on Cocos...
> In 1925, a New York Zoological Society oceanographic ship stopped at Cocos. Back in New York, expedition member Ruth Rose sought out Gissler, who was by then living in an apartment near the roaring trains of the El, "remembering tree ferns under a tropical moon, while he watches the flicker of an electric sign..." The scientists had visited Gissler's abandoned settlement at Wafer Bay, seen his decaying house. Now, Ruth Rose met a "big man, straight and upstanding as a youth, with a white beard that covered his chest, bright blue eyes that could twinkle or glower, and the shipshape trimness that speaks of seafaring..."

A decade after composing his meditation on this dive trip, the writer finds himself thinking of Gissler. Not Gissler on Cocos, but in New York City, near "the roaring trains of the El." Though nothing in Ruth Rose's anecdote suggests despair, when summoning Gissler's ghost the writer imagines a man whose dream is gone.

Conjuring Cocos: what the writer labored hardest at was describing the marine mayhem of hunter and hunted, as well as the diver-photographers' hunger to memorialize experience. All this he felt lucky to articulate. But, surprising the writer, not these concerns but Gissler's fate seems now to give him pause. As if, having survived the many predators at Cocos, and having made peace with the perhaps futile shipboard impulse to document or record—during or in place of experiences the divers were supposedly "having"—what the writer most fears is being washed ashore.

The writer wonders, Is that here, the cottage? If not, what has it been to him? Base camp: for what ascent? Way station: going where? Temporary housing, for thirty-one years? Default setting, to which he's reverted after the aberrations of travel? Training camp, writer/boxer in austere preparation? But then, where's the home he'll return to, and after what fight?

Such musings interrupted by a knock at the door. Who goes there? Dick's stopped by—"Good time?" he asks. Will accept half a shot of scotch. Among other things, Dick's a neighbor, also lawyer/climber/husband/raconteur/parent/reader/grandparent/friend. Collaborator with the writer in wry, unscheduled conversations about aging and the lives around them, this with banter about the point of it all. Dick: self-deprecating, honorable, often pellucid, drawing on books and songs he loves in order to illuminate what he needs to understand. A great capacity to lose his temper in confronting a wrong; an even greater capacity for forbearance.

This visit, he's brought the writer a Xerox of Ammons's "Clarity" (a one-sentence poem—sixty-something words, the writer concludes, if you count the ampersands). Initially, Ammons's narrator dazzlingly precises what might have caused the "rockslide" being contemplated, acknowledges it's a "pity" nothing now will be the same. But, the narrator goes on, something was "relieved," something revealed— "streaks & scores/of knowledge/now obvious and quiet."

As Dick sips his Lagavulin, the writer ponders the poem. "Wish I didn't know now what I didn't know then," Bob Seger sang in "Against the Wind." But Ammons's narrator argues even chaos can have eased "a bind," and, you get to know what you know. For all the good that'll do, the writer tells himself, sure Dick will smile, agree.

Late afternoon. The writer walks Dick out to the street. Amazing, the writer thinks, a life in which a friend brings such a poem by. And is, in part, living by such poems. The ordinary extraordinary. The writer reproaches himself for having deprecated life in the cottage.

They near Dick's station wagon. Oops, headlights on. Very Dick: some unfinished business, as the therapeutic community puts it, between him and cars.

"Don't even think about saying what you're thinking," Dick says to the writer, both of them laughing. Wanting to hear.

A friend calls, book of short stories recently published. "It's hard to figure the upside. Five years in the making, shat on by critics, no money in it, and my friends won't talk to me." Which puts the writer in mind of the joke about the Polish girl who wanted to be a movie star, went to Hollywood, started sleeping with writers. Still, he thinks, people seem to need to make books, even Salman Rushdie, who lamented there are too many being published while failing—of course—to curtail his own output.

Close to home, twenty-five books by the writer's mother came out in her lifetime, another eight posthumously, culled by the writer from a staggering array of manuscripts. Not long before she died, when a friend offered congratulations on yet one more, his mother set the Pollyanna straight: "I told her I write because I have to."

The writer's old friend Ken, great reader since college, his life at eighteen altered by encountering *Middlemarch,* calls to ask what's up. "Another book? You really are a writer," Ken enthuses. The writer bristles. How impede such undiscerning approval? Channeling his mother: "Ken, I rue the books I'd be reading were I not writing. You, reader, have the best of it."

"Say what you want," Ken replies, laughing, "you'll never stop writing."

Never stop writing? I could've stopped writing a million times, the writer thinks. And now? Now, I could *have* to stop writing. *Have* to stop? he asks himself. And why would that be? The writer makes a list.

- Physical effort required, keeping so many things in mind at once, "wrapping" one's mind around them, sustained focus, three years or more. Increasingly, bodily resistance to such demand. Or, say, writer as litmus paper, dunking himself in problems, solutions. Danger of drowning in such baptisms. Or…he thinks of Bob on his new Bobcat (sic) tractor, $35,000 tax-deductible skid-steer front-end loader with half-yard bucket and set of forklifts. Preparing to build a house on unstable landfill, Bob's at the helm, turning on a dime, moving earth for a retaining wall and piers going down eighteen feet. Writer doing his own somewhat less mechanized digging, digging.
- An understanding there's little time left to witness the evanescent creation the writer was born into, the one the old story says God authored. Writer tempted to try to take it on its own terms.
- Being unable to find his way back to the terrain of writing. No bread crumbs in this forest. How has he done it so many times? Solar reckoning, like migrating birds? Perhaps light is fading.
- Losing the capacity to live with imperfection, especially in early drafts. What confidence is required, tolerance. Like assuming the puppy will one day be housebroken.
- Many authors the writer knows are unable to publish. Sobering to see these…deaths. The writer's written only what he wanted, yet somehow been able to interface with book commerce. Just. Still, he's tired of the menace. Argument.
- A changed world. In his fiction seminar at the university one day, the writer thinks of his high school Latin teacher—hopelessly unfashionable, wearily aware that when he retires Latin will no longer be offered. The writer laughs: his brand of English a dead language! When author Cynthia Ozick rails against the

diminished status of fiction, the writer cannot but hear the self-interest. Also remembers the Greek gods: still referenced, but not much worshipped.

- What remains to be said. About error, wrong, aging, end of the self. The writer's not sure these are songs he wants to sing. Not what he had in mind when he "walked out one morning" long ago to tell stories about California's sixties in the vernacular of the Boston he was raised in.

So: this list. Then, already revising, the writer thinks of something to add.

- At the launch party for his third epigram book, he recounts to the audience his familiar feeling that in seeing a manuscript into print he's dodged another bullet. But also, now, that he feels like the woman in the carnival on the spinning wheel, arms and legs spread wide, knife thrower at work. Act done, the writer's outlined in knives, and, wow, no blood, no wounds. But it is strange and scary, the writer tells the audience, also true the wheel has stopped with him/her upside down.

In his late fifties, writer in Los Angeles to do radio and TV interviews, which soon pall. At a bookstore reading in Venice, a middle-aged woman comes up to him and says forthrightly, "You don't remember me, do you?" Amused, the writer starts a Search All in his mental computer: women he's dated, taught, danced salsa with; ex-wives of friends. Ex-wives of friends?

He stops the search. "No, sorry, I don't."

"Susan Stark."

The writer laughs. Now sees the girl within, classmate from grammar school. Bright, brash, witty, articulate. Still, as it turns out, great fun to banter with. As promised, she sends the writer a photo from eighth grade: 1957, four classmates. Sing now of the immortals: Stevie Lane, Bruce Sutton, Eddie Haven, Susan, and…the writer—taller at thirteen than the others, as he'd been for years. Looking, with Eisenhower jacket and khakis, hair cropped, like a young adult among teenagers. Diane Arbus's Jewish giant! The writer puts the snapshot on the bookcase near his desk, as if he'll figure out what to make of it.

The Internet. Soon after, he receives email from another grammar school classmate, this time with the 1957 graduation photo, boys in coat and tie. An upwelling of familiar linked syllables: *Pen-el-o-pe Ryan. Herbie Goines, Al-bie Pres-ton, A-my Na-ples.* Names, memory flashes. Joel Galway, always anxious, his incredible collection of adventure biographies—Davy Crockett, Wild Bill Hickok,

Jim Bridger—coveted by the writer as young reader. Mikey Conrad's many enormous knives (Mikey a virgin male, like all of them). Dolly Fleming, tap dancing in yet another class play, forlorn in spangles and crinoline. Eddie Haven's aged grandparents, his father occasionally visiting. Luke Sand's virtuosity on the trumpet. The funeral of Eugene Evan's mother. (Not in the photo, Chloe, with whom at eleven he played spin-the-bottle, just the two of them. Where did she go, when?) Writer at his desk in the cottage, studying this picture of classmates he mostly forgot. Worked to forget?

Grammar school. Shinnying up the rope in gym class. Seventh-grade teacher Mrs. Gray, her appetite for apple polishers. Mr. Law, shop teacher, incredulous the writer had so little mechanical aptitude. The stories one tells oneself: well aware it's story told long after the fact, still the writer (increasingly?) recalls those years as bleak. On visits back to Boston in his thirties, he'd return to the grammar school, walking the route taken as a child, as if there was something to be reconstructed, as if he might summon up words to describe what he recalled as oppressive. Once in a great while, in a dream, a place recurs in his memory: by an apartment building next to the school's tar tennis courts. Bare ground/no walls. A hideout, yes, but why so vivid? Where he and his friends smoked cigarettes, played with matches? The writer waits for answers. Nothing. Nothing beyond memory of so many desultory hours around the schoolyard, nothing happening. Nothing at home except more lessons, discipline. Lots of rule breaking, lies, getting caught. Just plain sad, or Seasonal Affective Disorder? Endless early winter, late winter, perennially "late" spring. Class photo: makes the writer sad. Something stunted about all of them. "Pellagra," the writer says aloud. Laughs. Word learned as a child from a lyric by satirist Tom Lehrer.

In this period, one of the writer's grammar school classmates starts to correspond. Brave, intelligent, she's recently survived being a patient at the cancer center his father dreamed and brought into being. His father's hospital when he was young; the dying children. Part of the oppressive memory? His father's other children? How little his father was home, dedicated to his great lifework while coping with his own debility. The writer's mother's frequent use of the word *privilege* to describe the children's "opportunities." Her message, unspoken, that the world was hostile: one had to excel, while protecting the family's reputation. It was all about control (Boston so small, riddled with class and ethnic discriminations, so mean-spirited). At home, in any case, any doubt about being entitled—were the neighbors' children really so hapless, were they not more free to play?—was mocked as self-pity. And love? Nothing unconditional about it.

Where the writer grew up. When he's sixty, his friend Andrea, visiting Boston, goes to see it. Takes pictures—of the house, street signs: Amory, corner of Freeman. (No polyamory on Amory, the writer's younger sister observes, so much not-free on Freeman.) Childhood: once more in the back door, singing out, "I'm home; anybody home?"

Studying photos Andrea brings to the cottage, the writer asks himself what he cherished as a boy, what obsessed him. Besides Chloe and spin-the-bottle? His father's hug, kiss on forehead. Football with his brother; spiral after spiral. Sledding in Amory Park. Brigham's sundaes, fudge and marshmallow. *Marshmallow?* Joe and Nemo's franks in Kenmore Square near Fenway Park, mustard and the almost-too-sweet relish he…relished. "Jotto," written word-guessing game played with his siblings. Lobster and French fries; popovers! Richard Halliburton's *Book of Marvels* again, again. The word *bosom* in Pyle's *The Merry Adventures of Robin Hood*. The vast emptiness and unheated chill of white-walled squash courts at the Harvard Club, fat old man downstairs, aged turtle head poking out of a steam cabinet's carapace. Riding his bike—the Schwin, the Dawes—to Irving's Variety Store for red licorice, nonpareils. The disturbingly too-powerful wisteria climbing up the side of the house by the music room, something out of "Jack and the Beanstalk."

The lingua franca of his young male friends. Saying to someone who asked you to play basketball: "Let's not and say we did." To someone approaching you and a friend: "Two's company, three's a crowd." Or, "Why don't you go play in traffic?" To someone blocking your view: "You make a better door than a window." To someone irritating you or not irritating you: "Sit on my finger and rotate and tell me when you reach my elbow." Or, "Eat shit and die." To someone who asked where you'd been: "If I'd been up your ass, you'd know." To someone foolish enough to ask any question at all: "That's for me to know and you to find out." Inky-dinky *parlez vous*. As regards the weather, that endless gray low overhead/sweltering summer/interminable winter, it was "a fuckin' joke" or "shitty."

Or was it? There is the prospective, and there is the retrospective. Draaisma argues that "old age seems to write itself into the memories of youth." How, then, test memory? Well, as the writer and his childhood friends would sing when they thought someone was exaggerating or lying, "In Mexico, they sling the bull, but someone does it here." Still, there's that line at the end of *Lear*, the king having—so royally—fucked up, when Albany tells Kent and Edgar they must "Speak what we feel, not what we ought to say."

The past, revisited. Humiliations, we're told, have the longest atomic half-life. Memory, as the idiom goes, refreshed.

erena's son Billy comes over, boy the writer helped raise now a young man. Handsome, affable, good with people. Wanting feedback on a community college term paper about evolutionary biologist Stephen Jay Gould. Paper's OK: having returned to school after dropping out, Billy's learning to marshal his arguments. And this is a long way from his volcanic teen years, bitter contempt for book learning. What a misery that was: divorced by Serena for "domestic violence" and alcoholism when Billy was three, Billy's father set his star on undermining whatever she wanted, including (academic) success for their son. Perhaps also he was jealous of his boy's possibilities, wanted to see him fail as he had. Realized if his son could think clearly he'd see his old man for what he was.

Marshaling arguments. In California's family court system, unless a parent is doing physical violence to a child, both parents have equal say on everything. In adjacent Oregon, however, if the parents cannot generally agree, the court chooses a primary custodian. For years, Billy's mother and the writer believed if they conveyed to the family court what was going on, the court would have to be supportive. Over and again, the writer presented arguments in letters to court counselors, therapists, judges, sure they would intervene.

Billy, his term paper. Billy's getting more sophisticated at ordering his ideas, and the writer tells him the skill is essential no matter what kind of work he goes into. Does not, however, also explain to Billy just how little practical effect the written word can have.

And what else might the writer now tell Billy? Well, he could give him Grace Paley's "A Conversation with My Father," call-and-response between father and daughter about human capacity for change, the nature of narrative. Just when do stories achieve a final version? Don't we rush to preclude possibility?

Some months after that term paper, Billy drops out of college a second time. Another failure, or healthy impulse for a truer life? Aberrant episode? Determinative? The writer remembers blindly leaving Yale Law School after a week—couldn't face three more years of lonely schoolwork; loathed New Haven; had a girlfriend back in Cambridge. Even his Contracts professor seemed envious as he departed, but of course the writer had to live his "freedom."

The writer worries for Billy. Tries not to factor in his vivid memory of worry for himself at that age. Interrogates the narrative he's constructing. Wishes he could fast-forward, have the relief of knowing Billy's story has a happy ending.

I solation tank: you float in a solution of Epsom Salt, "in the silence of a weightless world, free of distractions." Good, the maker says, for stress reduction, weight management, chronic fatigue, endorphin production. Isolation cells, on the other hand, are a form of punishment. Tanks, cells: if the writer has long erred on the side of being able to think his own thoughts, the clarity of quiet, there are downside risks. *Alone:* from Middle English, all—wholly—one.

Winter coming on, inexorable wheel of the seasons. Writer, a party of wholly one, in the cottage listening to Leonard Cohen. Can Leonard help, his self-indulgent melancholy, often lugubrious lyrics with—facile—gloom of having again fallen from the grace of love? Sensing the end even as love began. But at times, Leonard has the power: wry knowingness transmuted into wisdom, loss into appreciation. In "Alexandra Leaving," transforming a Cavafy poem Cohen admonishes the bereft not to choose a "coward's explanation," not to stoop to argue "the moment was imagined."

Writer home alone, brooding. As it happens, his grim mood has a destination. He's time-traveling to *Great Expectations,* both Dickens novel and the 1940s film, when orphan Pip encounters wealthy Miss Havisham. Curtains drawn against the light of day, room illuminated by candles, young Pip sees "the bride within the bridal dress had withered like the dress, and like the flowers, and had no brightness left but the brightness of her sunken eyes." Jilted, embittered Miss

Havisham, clocks arrested at the moment of humiliation. Memory of whom suddenly makes the writer laugh. One's inner Miss Havisham? Cottage as her mansion?

The bed downstairs. The writer's *inamorata* sprawls, likes to sprawl, in her sleep. A problem solver, he bought lumber, took out saw and screwdriver, expanded the wooden frame, shopped for a larger mattress. Wonders now if he should now cut the bed back down to size.

Moving on. Or not. When the writer's six, the family makes a long stay in Mexico City—his pathologist-father consulting at the Hospital Infantil, the children attending the bilingual Colegio Americano. As an adult, the writer takes occasional vacations in Mexico, mostly Baja, drawing on shards of Spanish learned as a child and in a high school summer class, drawing also on cognates from Latin and his more adequate French. Though he says he cannot speak Spanish despite easy use of *algunas palabras*, it seems something he *could* do well, may get to when less consumed by his mother tongue. Though, on the other hand, time is getting short(er).

As the writer begins to immerse himself in salsa, of course he feels bad about lyrics he barely gets the gist of, sometimes goes online to look them up, deciphering the Spanish or finding an English translation. Or, setting a song on endless loop, track repeating, repeating, the writer waits for Spanish to manifest itself as a unified whole. *Corazon, amor, la vida*, and then…fluency by osmosis. But, truth be told, the writer doesn't entirely mind what he's missing: the absence of words focuses him on the music's polyrhythms, about which he has so much to learn.

Beyond this, however, when the writer starts salsa, he feels done with words for the moment or, even, that words have led him astray.

Pursuit of story often removed him from the larger world. Not that the writer reproaches himself: it was a risk in the effort to do something well, make it true. There's being intoxicated by narrative, then there's being fixated on creating it. How pursue something halfway? Though the writer's *inamorata* wants to write fiction, though academia's what she calls her day job, even as she admires the writer's discipline she thinks he's taken it too far. Or, perhaps, that he's too taken with it to give her the attention she requires. So if for the writer dance now displaces language, being an apostate to what he's most skilled at seems a not entirely bad thing.

Words. One day the writer's listening and air-salsaing to Eliades Ochoa's rollicking *"Estoy como nunca"* ("Never been better"). It's the opening cut on the CD, and, smitten since first hearing it, he's yet to get past it. But that morning, putting things in place around the cottage, he lets the CD play. And then, as if he'd been waiting for it all along, there's the remarkable final track.

> *Sus ojos se cerraron,*
> *y el mundo sigue andando,*
>
> Her eyes have closed,
> and the world keeps going.

A ballad, Ochoa's acoustic guitar and solo voice. What a distance between the album's first and last cuts—from group to individual, exultation to lament. The lyrics are by poet Alfredo Le Pera, collaborator of legendary singer Carlos Gardel before both died in a plane crash in 1935. It's not hard to pick out words—*tormento, lamento, dolor*—but the writer asks a friend to translate. Over and again, track repeating, the writer's lost in the bitter last lines.

El carnaval del mundo
gozaba y se reía,
burlándose el destino
me robó su amor.

And meanwhile in the streets
with insane babbling
the carnival of the world enjoyed itself and laughed
mocking the destiny
that robbed me of her love.

Language. Often, CD's playing for hours, air salsa in the living room is a kind of tarantella, dancer either driven mad by or seeking to purge the spider's venom. Venom? What a word: pure poison. Think, say, disbelief. Self-reproach: his *inamorata* feared the writer's "splendid isolation," his not-desperate-enough need.

In the writer's dialogue with her—sophisticated reader, skilled story-teller—communion through and across language is manifest; beyond such oral and aural sex, she's offered to be the writer's (one) true reader. Yet now, language—the writer's passion, faith, his...very self—*language* keeps failing him. Argument and pleading, pleading and argument incapable of bringing her back—home?—to the cottage.

I n the late 1980s, part-time resident of Hawaiʻi and looking for the words to describe (warm) ocean, the writer became obsessed with the emerging post-colonial fiction of the South Pacific. In these very small island nations, the writer found in his travels, indigenous author and reader were never far removed from each other. Albert Wendt and Epeli Hauʻofa, for instance, needed courage to be the first to expose "family" secrets or publish satire. More than a decade later, Samoan writer Fia Sigiel, soon to be celebrated in many countries and languages, experienced not unwarranted anxiety about reaction at home to her first book. Long since, the writer himself had felt apprehensive about the response of family, friends, lovers—about his own response!—to his books, such powerful magic invoked. But as he wandered in the South Pacific, he could see the very practical imperative of this new fiction, the saying of essential truths where public narratives had long been controlled by those with religious or political power.

In Berkeley in the late 1990s, the writer had a student, Gulf War veteran writing fiction about the violent barrio of his childhood. One day, the student explained his doubts about the social value of books, as opposed, say, to working with troubled kids at juvenile hall.

"Well, what's the value to the community of Garcia Marquez's *One Hundred Years of Solitude?*" the writer asked, and they both laughed.

When the student completed a book-length manuscript, the writer offered to send it to his agent and editor, but the student had already decided not to publish, not even pseudonymously. Perhaps he felt too implicated in the book's violence, or that the book's content might hamper his ambitions in other métiers.

This student's decision, and the apprehension of Sia Figiel, the writer thought, were in part a struggle with the question of what Buddhists term right speaking. Or, as the Talmudists call it, *lashon hara*. Negative or disparaging speech: the evil tongue, sin of gossip, and slanderous talk. A defiling of the mouth, tongue for good reason behind a wall of teeth; tongue as razor. Tale bearing, evil talk, untrue statements, all are prohibited. Further, it can be a violation to say "anything about another person, even if it is true, even if it is not negative, even if it is not secret, even if it hurts no one, even if the person himself would tell the same thing if asked [jewfaq.org]." Gossip, for instance, "kills three: the person who speaks it, the person who hears it, and the person about whom it is told," and "It is forbidden to even imply or suggest negative things about a person." There are exceptions, but the thrust of Jewish law is to equate tale bearing with murder, adultery, and idol worship. A desecration of the name of G_d, it cuts the offender off from the world to come.

As Mordecai Silver puts it, "If you don't have something nice to say about someone, then don't say it at all! And this includes even thinking about it." *Even thinking about it.* But how we humans do seem to think about it. Seem also to interrogate even divinely inspired narratives of social control. Resist the priestly caste's inability to discriminate between, say, skilled and unskilled gossip. And then someone, it appears, is forever doomed and determined to say the emperor has no clothes.

So, writer as murderer/adulterer/idol worshipper, precluded from the world to come. Our present talebearer's sole flirtation with organized religion was several months of a charismatic Gurdgieff teacher's weekend meetings in 1967. Quitting the company of hundreds of exultant seekers hungry to free themselves from a blind state of "recurrence," sorry to resume fulltime life among those who were "asleep," the writer told himself he'd chosen Chaucer. ("What was he smoking?" you may inquire.) He thought to describe the sometimes wondrous, sometimes craven lives of fellow fallen creatures would be a high calling. And demanding. He'd already sensed most truths are partial, and that a proponent's advocacy could contain more self-interest than self-knowledge. This the writer garnered both from skepticism in his mother's milk and from struggling to parse the obvious, that his exemplary parents could not (be thought to) possess all that would have to govern his life. Or, as some California Buddhists seem to cherish saying, the writer had to kill his parents (then his teacher and the Buddha).

As it turns out, one recurrence in the writer's life has been a mild exposure to Buddhism. During the 1970s and '80s in northern California, Buddhism was never far from being referenced. Was, in some circles, a kind of state quasi-religion. You climbed in Yosemite/could surf/were pro-choice/against war/had been to Zen centers at Tassajara, Green Gulch. Buddhism inflected the cultural conversation as Freud had in the late fifties and early sixties, nothing then not wish fulfillment or repressed. In college, the writer devoured Freud, later learned much from psychoanalyst-essayists (but never went into therapy, as perhaps he should have). Nor, despite decades in California, has he been a Buddhist. In the writer's childhood, the Boston triumvirates of rabbi, minister, and priest—obligatory opening act for public functions—seemed pompous, hypocritical, denying sexuality, crippled by solemnity. Sanctified: equaled sanctimonious. Decades later, there was no surprise for the writer in the sexual indiscretions of then-famous Baker Roshi of the San Francisco Zen Center (kids, never, ever trust a honkey who calls himself Roshi); in Trungpa Rinpoche's stimulant-abetted abuses in Colorado (Allen Ginsberg shamefully loath to disavow them); or in the dissimulations of Richard Alpert/Ram Dass (actually, no stigmata in his guru's hands, but hey, no biggie). Such self-aggrandizement: who'd have presumed these prelates immune from the "spiritual materialism" they seemed to lick their lips to describe. Or perhaps they were victims: how resist the credulity of the infantilized faithful? Also, the writer was put off by Zen tales of monks trumping one another in verbal sparring. Facile with words (and future epigrammist), he doubted scoring of points provoked or manifested illumination.

But what do foibles of the professionally religious have to do with religion? Buddhism has been important to a number of the writer's friends who center themselves in meditation, aspire to compassionate contemplation—and perhaps transcendence—of our common experience of thwarted need, suffering, death. Young Max, for instance, who helped the writer after his heart operation. Their "walking meditations" in the neighborhood: this butterfly, that flower—what *was* the hurry? Yes, going for coffee, but who needed to get there? Max also had an engaging self-deprecation. As one of his raps goes, "Ever since my satori I've been mired in delusion."

Faith. In that milk of the writer's matter-of-factly agnostic, lover-and-transmuter-of-Bible-stories mother (*How the Left-Behind Beasts*

Built Ararat; All Those Mothers at the Manger; etc.), he imbibed a...gospel, hunger to celebrate the miraculous in the material. His mother closely observing and articulating the specific; hard-won language as song, this with mandarin reluctance to say that's what one was doing. But what, then, of young Max's satori? The enlightenment experience; a glimpse of oneness. The yearning to get beyond death and the suffering of reincarnation. Maybe the writer intuited his task was not to cure or transcend, but—merely—to transmute, reveal. Or maybe, All-American Jewish country boy from Boston, maybe the writer simply was not afraid for his soul or fate. Just enjoyed mastering the capacity to describe life's confusions, the way some writers in the 1950s avoided psychotherapy lest, "cured," they'd lose the capacity to write.

Say, then, that the writer kinda believed he *could* be improved by Buddhism but was, yes, *attached* to the writer's manias. He gave up the omnipresent marijuana by his late twenties, walked away from cocaine (for which he never paid, despite a gift for consuming it) with no more than nostalgia. And while he overcame his addiction to tobacco at thirty-six, cold turkey—after a Gold Medal in smoking in the Olympics—he stuck with, was stuck in, storytelling.

Story. Everybody, the writer felt, had a faith—a story—subsuming everyone else's. Blind, often, to its partiality, how it diminished life's teeming multiplicities in favor of liberating insight. Not seeing it might be self-serving. Freud's story (but could Freud party?). Marx's story. Stories by the priests of this god, that. People seemed to select one universalizing narrative or another. The one they were good at, most favored by? Politicians, the politician story (they say Washington is Hollywood for uglies). Buddhists, the Buddha story, which may have been the most comfortable or compelling tale for a sensitive prince whose mother died a week after he was born, who had thirty-two nurses to raise him, who without a word of farewell left wife and child to do—like, say, Shane, or like the other restless young men of his own time—what he had to do. So much for being a householder, even as future king! Who later stayed on the road to transmit what he was sure he'd learned about how to be. What, he was sure, no one of his epoch had learned.

And the writer? Turns out he had a story called literature, a way of knowing that subsumed other ways of knowing. Subsumed as characters—as individual, fallible human beings—the practitioners of all faiths, systems. In the 1960s, marijuana made vital for him an old trope: they *were* players on a stage, *were* the archetypes. He'd play the writer. Sentence of hard labor on sentences, it would keep him busy: he'd sing the song of their lives.

Berkeley, 2005. Summertime, 30,000 students vaporized till late August, the credentialing Cuisinart replaced by unused parking spaces and morning fog. Within one week, the writer receives two tickets from underemployed motorcycled police—oh macho mirrored sunglasses, black leather boots!—for not buckling up: $195.00 each. "Click it or ticket." "Fuck it or suck it," the writer muttered. Recurrence. En route to being twice apprehended in this way, he was thinking about Buddhism. Looked up the word *avatar* (Sanskrit: descent, as of a deity), Afro-Cuban music on the stereo, occasionally leaving the computer for some salsa steps. As a Buddhist-Catholic-Jewish friend recommended, he picked up a copy of *After the Ecstasy, the Laundry: How the Heart Grows Wise on the Spiritual Path.* Seeing the accompanying jacket image—pastoral setting, laundry line, no washing machine—the writer pondered what the designer intended to convey about the author. Well, surely not a child molester. Since Buddhist teachers seem—like most authors—driven to more than one book, the writer thought of a possible sequel: *My Dirty Laundry: Soiled; Sold.* The cover graphic would be graphic.

"All right, Tommy," the writer admonished himself. The writer's friend Andrea had been calling him Tommy the last several years, first person since grade school to do so, and he'd adopted her mode when speaking to himself.

"Tommy, listen, your spiritual practice is to note your impatience with this kind of tripe and get past it." He remembered the 1980s, when California Buddhists (dis!)honored the word *honor* to death. Now, eyeing the book jacket, the words *unctuous/cloying/oleaginous* occurred to him. Mindfully, as he'd heard so many northern Californians say, he paid dispassionate attention, let them go. Turned to page 299, read the author's acknowledgements: "First, I offer a bow of true gratitude…" The writer breathed deep, listened to his breath. Shat a brick. Just my fucking luck, he thought, fucked over by a fucking adjective. *True* just too true, immediately invoking its opposite.

What was the writer so *not* mindfully arguing here? That language and essence are related? Not "You are what you eat," but "You are what you say"? That smarmy/teacher's pet/brown-nosing language means a smarmy, teacher's pet brown-noser? That assertions of sincerity—including his own, he cautioned himself—kill the soul, damage the souls of others? G_d help him, that's what the writer was saying. "Right speech": Buddha's admonition to refrain from lies, slander, and idle chatter, read by one commentator as telling the truth, speaking gently, and talking only when necessary. Then, this fellow's book? "Sorry," the writer muttered. "Not necessary."

Young Max had turned the writer on to fifteenth-century Zen poet Ikkyu, who, unattached as anyone could be, was nonetheless survived by many poems, acolytes, the great love he met at seventy-four when she was twenty-five, and himself as legend. One of his poems reads:

> Writing something
> To leave behind
> Is yet another kind of dream:
> When I awake I know that
> There will be no one to read it.

Which, five centuries later, the writer read. Back in the mid-1980s, taking stock of his vocation, turning forty in the wake of his mother's death, ready to appraise what he'd made of himself, the writer came across an interview with Arthur Koestler. "I must have had something to say," Koestler told the interviewer, referring to his thirty books. Subsequently committing joint suicide with his third wife.

In this period, Bob calls. New home he and his wife, Colette, built recently finished, another amazing work of skill and care. Their previous house now sold, receiving great praise. His business, as he turns seventy-two, booming. Still not bidding jobs: time and materials. The writer teases Bob his contracting formula will be his epitaph.

Though Bob and Colette sometimes keep their distance from people, they love animals, are sickened by humans who harm them. One of their cats, which has slept on Bob's pillow for fifteen years, is ill; Bob has been administering insulin, gently force-feeding. Finally, it's time to bring in a vet to help the cat die. Today, next week? Delay for whose benefit? The cat gazes at Bob as it has for so many years. Inquiring, perhaps, if Bob too is ready to let go.

Death in the air. Wife of an old friend of the writer, wonderful woman, early fifties, liver cancer. Neighbor with cataracts. Old and poor in wheelchairs on the roadside after Hurricane Katrina. War victims in Iraq. When the writer was a child, he and his siblings would sing, "The worms crawl in/The worms crawl out/The worms play pinochle/On your snout." Sang this with glee. Less gleeful now, the writer compensates with his own kind of religion. Yet again recalls that, asked if narration was dead, Bernard Malamud replied, "It'll be dead when the penis is." For a line like which the writer has—say it loud!—*true* gratitude. In a world of relentless flux, he builds his house on the rock of such talk.

Attach. To nail to. To crave, wish, want, long for. *Desire,* from the Latin, *desiderare* (to await) from the stars.

Andrea's photographs of the cottage, what strikes her playful, incisive eye:

- Woodblock under bathroom window. Modest, practical, also allowing sight of the neighbor's black bamboo.
- Spareness of the downstairs bedroom shot into mirror on white wall. Bed with striped blanket, reversed, in reflection. Color!
- Living room—austere, to Andrea. Tightly woven sisal rug, overlaying overlaid oblongs of sunlight.
- Upstairs on the window sill, very close up, the writer's shot glass of fine scotch—half empty; half full? Five almost animate roasted almonds (unsalted).
- Photo of the attic, lens making it large, serene. The upstairs the writer always wanted! And another shot, pony wall door open to reveal a tumult of book boxes under the eaves. Andrea amused by the (backstage) chaos.
- Outside, beside the house, Katrin's emergency cider jugs of water by the fence, still there after…thirty years. Roadside shrine?
- Shelf of books in the study. Colors, titles, the writer's footsteps: *Porn Studies*, *The History of Hell*, *The Theatre of Don Juan*, *The Dyer's Hand*.
- Above the phone table in the hall, cluster of stamped tin images—heart, eyes, ship, hands in prayer—from Greece in the early 1970s. Also Saint George slaying a dragon, and a card of young Maher Baba looking a bit like the writer in the 1960s.
- Shot from the living room into the downstairs bedroom. Bare

wood floor, white walls, and, on the handle of the study door, industrial sound protectors, black with vivid red outlining. Photographer taking the measure of all the writer seeks to exclude.

Camera at the ready, Andrea drops by, as she often does, sits with the writer on the loveseat in the living room alcove (Arabic, *al-quobbah*). She's brought a portfolio of new prints, also needs his response to the latest crisis with John.

"Tommy, am I a drama queen?" Question she's no doubt already put to therapist, girlfriends, co-workers, former spouse—Andrea's marvelous, well-deserved support system.

The writer can see how one might think so, but the phrase doesn't catch the persistently volatile dynamic she and John have…constructed? Fallen into? Refused to correct? All-too-human, he feels, remembering one folly or another he's lived. Some months before, Andrea brought John by, poor John, to hear the writer's calmly dour assessment, which neither had trouble disregarding as they thanked him, went out the front gate. Another time, John came over on his own. To see Andrea's very close friend for advice? Nodded thoughtfully at each point the writer made about how the relationship had been doomed by John's inexplicable behavior—more than once he failed to show up for a date or dinner with Andrea. Just plain forgetful—though, as the writer noted, John did keep his motorcycle in good shape. John high-mindedly averring he'd let Andrea go, this being the best thing for her. And then, apologetically, answering his cell phone: *Yes, Andrea!* Heading over to her place for more of the same. Writer thinking Jim Morrison: "Don't you love her madly, don't you love her as she's walkin' out the door." Wisdom the writer acquired from his own life's first-hand—as they term it—experience.

Andrea in the cottage, where she's sung along with Queen's over-the-top "Bohemian Rhapsody," with Leonard Cohen's "Famous Blue Raincoat." Where she's patiently partnered salsa as the writer worked out a turn. Now, narrating the latest installment of the John saga, simultaneously distraught and laughing at herself, Andrea asks about the writer's new book. This book. Fetching the typescript from the study, the writer sits down next to her, looks for a section she hasn't heard. They've been doing this for a year, Andrea requesting, listening. Reminding the writer of 1967, phoning his friend Terry when he first began weekly underground newspaper pieces, exuberantly reading Terry another story-in-progress. The writer, now, leafing pages, feeling oddly unprepared as he bumps into one section, another, each suddenly vivid, hyper-real. Then reaching an early version of Dick coming by with the Ammons poem.

When the writer finishes, Andrea says, "Oh, Tommy, this is wonderful, it's going to be your best book."

This the writer doubts, but then again, knows it's just too soon to tell.

The present: life between the still-to-come and the unable-to-remember. The writer's doctor friend has a mother-in-law with Alzheimer's. Her past, here-and-now, and future encompass two minutes. The writer's friend thinks of her as trapped in this condition, but, thoughtfully, adds that it does have "low morbidity." (*Morbid,* heard when the writer was a child—e.g., "Don't be morbid," or, "a morbid sense of humor.")

Memory. And memory, triggered. In the front yard, the white lawn chairs. Seeing them one afternoon, the writer remembers being there twenty years before. He's in his late thirties then, single. Is having coffee with a woman just getting clear of a humiliating marriage. Mary. As they sit in the sun, she describes her husband's crudeness, infidelities, browbeating, her credulousness, submissiveness. Shame.

"Does that turn you off?" she asks, studying the writer's face.

Mary explains she married right after college to avoid having to go home to live with her parents. Her mother was ill; her parents needed help. She couldn't stand the thought of returning to that small town in the Central Valley. Only marriage could exempt her. She didn't know her husband-to-be all that well, but he very much wanted her. Never did she expect to pay so much for any decision. Thinks perhaps in a previous life she did something terribly wrong.

"Like what?" the writer asks.

"I think I killed a sea turtle, a beautiful sea turtle, hundreds of years old. I had a dream about it. A nightmare."

The first time they sleep together, upstairs in the attic, Mary asks him to teach her how to please him. "Show me," she says. Beseeches. Implores.

The next morning, the writer goes to the dictionary. *Implorare:* Latin, to cry, cry out, invoke with tears. *Explore,* he learns, is to cry out at the moment of discovery.

After they've been seeing each other for several weeks, as they drive home after dinner in a Chinese restaurant, Mary hugs him, says, "I'll die if you leave me."

The white lawn chairs in the yard, twenty years later. Thinking not about, say, Katrin and her three cats lying there in the sun, but Mary. Thinking also of a pop song from when the writer was a child: "Mem-o-ries"—three very slow syllables—"are made of this."

The garage-library. Plywood floors with clear polyurethane finish over two-by-four sleepers nailed into the concrete; unfinished floor-to-ceiling bookcases lining the walls. Bob's inexpensive, elegant design. No first editions, but, for the writer, a treasure house.

Reading the news one morning, the writer learns that a man in New York City was smothered—died of suffocation—when one of his bookcases fell over. Out in the garage-library later that day, the writer experiences an access of shedding. Books on the stock market *(A Fool and His Money);* countless anthologies of short stories, complimentary from publishers; mid-twentieth-century tomes on rural Ireland, picked up there in 1974 on a trip with Katrin; *Back to Eden* and others of her sixties cookbooks. He places them in a cardboard box, puts it out on the tree lawn. The writer's making clear to himself he doesn't intend to write about the dotcom mania; feels he knows what he needs to know about the range of short fiction; will keep only the work of writers he savors; will never get to write about Ireland; that his diet is as healthy as he can…stand. So, relief, books gone. Which leaves? Shelves and shelves of different alphabets: sex and death; Hawai'i; the South Pacific; fiction and some literary nonfiction; writing and the writer's life; surfing; ocean; nature writing; epigrams and lying; Boston and New England; California and the sixties. And shelves with book clusters. Fairy tales/myths/children's stories (toward retelling the story of Cupid and Psyche?). Cuba and

Afro-Cuban music. Judaica. Truth commissions. Versions of the Don Juan story.

Almost immediately, the writer rues putting out the box, goes back to check titles. Convinces himself, just, not to retrieve the books. God, he thinks, what must it have been like for bibliophile Walter Benjamin, German Jew fleeing Paris as the Nazis arrived. Leaving his library behind, carrying the manuscript of his magnum opus. Soon, trapped, to commit suicide. As Jay Parini renders it, Benjamin wrote, "Death is what sanctions everything the storyteller can tell. Indeed, he borrows his authority from death."

Storytelling: whatever its animus, for the writer it's an inherited gene. Lares and penates: beneficent ancestral spirits, schoolboy Latin, part of the lingua franca when the writer was young. In the cottage's study, the writer has his lares and penates on the bookshelf: copy of the *Boston Globe* editorial on his father's death—"medical legend…legend in his lifetime." And, beside the row of his mother's thirty-plus books, pictures of his parents: together, separately. In one photograph, his mother, seventy, holds a copy of her recently published *How Does It Feel to Be Old?* (1979), in which the narrator says to her granddaughter,

> Have you noticed, I'm shorter, almost than you?
> I'm shrinking, you're stretching. What else is new?
> Well, sun keeps rising,
> journeys of planets continue exact.
> Wind keeps blowing,
> sky stays wide.

In this photograph, playing the grande dame, the writer's mother has gathered herself—level gaze for the camera, slight smile, eyebrows slightly raised. She has four years to live.

The writer's father died in 1973. Grieving, the writer's mother composes *Year of Reversible Loss,* Basho-like poetry and prose, endeavoring by very close—desperate—observation of the natural world to make a case for the continuity of matter. Of love. How, she wondered, how affirm dissolution.

Of the many books that followed during her next—last—ten years, one was *Something Further...* Its author's bio note, which she composed, read in part:

> Wife, mother, widow, grandmother: Norma Farber considers these characterizations her leading roles.
> Additionally she has enacted actress, concert singer, poet, translator, author of books for children.

The provenance of the book's title is the finale of Melville's *The Confidence Man*: "Something further may follow of this masquerade." In the 132-line title poem, the poet argues that in both natural and human worlds all is disguise. The sun a masquerader—as if it cared about our survival! Genesis a divine performance, and, given the changes of, say, the molting dragonfly, then "Where's that insect essence?" Leading the poet to posit that "who you are, is less/than how you play." Finally, the poem concludes, "I mask/my soul, and subterfuge/invites the show to follow." Readers left to ponder just what a show is—revelation; deception; display? And to wonder what is that something that may follow this masquerade. From time to time the writer takes *Something Further...* down from the shelf, rereads the poem, always disturbed by it, feeling it somehow eludes him, or is trying to tell him something he's not eager to know.

Da capo: Italian, from the beginning; repeat. From the sheet music of the writer's childhood. Stories he tells now, has told before. Looking for what? Raised by a stage-door mother, as a child the writer's mother excelled in an endless round of lessons—ballet, singing, elocution, piano, languages—while envisioning escape from that overwhelming empowerer. At eighteen, against her mother's wild subversions, she married a brilliant young doctor, then never, ever again saw or corresponded with her mother. This while as lieder singer and actress she became very much the performer her mother had had in mind: "Elegance, intelligence, refinement and subtlety" *(Cleveland Plain Dealer);* "masterful" *(Christian Science Monitor);* "tour de force" *(Boston Globe).*

Social roles. Boston, where the writer's mother lived her entire life, really was a little England: status- and class-ridden; you knew your station. And when the writer's father became world famous, there was the role of consort, an impeccability to insist on. Audience: Boston a kind of panopticon. And, inevitably, medical politics—critics; rivals.

Widow on display. In the high-rise near Harvard Square, full of local luminaries, you perforce presented a self on the elevator or passing the front desk in the lobby. Gossip and *schadenfreude* to stave off; secrets to keep. Groundlings insinuating. So many permeable membranes. All this was strenuous, requiring sustained resolve. Or perhaps, having lost the love of her life, the writer's mother now had only stage presence to hold herself together.

The past, where, Ross McDonald wrote, "crucial events and conversations of our lives repeat themselves forever in the hope of being understood and perhaps forgiven." The dying of the writer's mother: during her terminal illness, attended to by her four children, she had no apologies to make. If one of her "leading roles" was "mother," in that life script she could not but "follow," the line "I love you" was nowhere to be found. Surely she had her reasons—that mother who taught her to avoid (cheap, manipulative) sentiment at any cost. Still, the writer had imagined there were things she'd try to set straight, take back, reconcile, with one or another of her grown children. To help them free themselves. How could someone so phenomenally articulate remain so mute? But no, no such impulse, capacity. Or was it, *no such generosity, grace?* The writer's disturbed by these words, says them to himself twenty-something years later, knowing they're going to feel unfair, wrong. What he and his siblings experienced back then was compassion for their mother's suffering; guilt that they could not save her; grieving for impending loss. Nor did it seem conceivable to do less than care for her as their father would have wanted. Endeavoring to be gallant in her dying, in any case, playing her part, cherished privacy gone, their mother suffered the good intentions of the physicians, former pupils of her late husband, whose ministrations only prolonged her misery. What a game!

Books: running in the family. The writer's mother gave him a copy of *Something Further...*, inscribed it, "For Tom—this Masquerade." Telling her son what? The writer rereads to weigh who she was. To see himself in her, or not. Risky, such revisiting. This posthumous conversation, his mother reminding him—chiding, rebuking, reproving—from the Far Side that the dead are at the mercy of the living. "Do with me what you will," she says. Laughs: "Your failure to grasp this slays me. What do you think *your* books are? *Do I make myself clear?*" Demanding assent, as always when she disciplined her young children, but as if he'll never/ever figure it out. Which leaves the writer wondering, What work of the art she lived by is she referencing from out there in the Great Beyond? The writer takes a shot at it. Yeats, maybe, on Cordelia/Lear/Ophelia/Hamlet: "if worthy their prominent part in the play [they] do not break up their lines to weep."

Lares and penates, continued. On a bookshelf in the writer's study there's a photograph of his father with German pathologist Ludwig Pick. May 1932: the writer's father is twenty-eight, Instructor in Pathology at Harvard Medical School. Smiling, vital, at ease in a rumpled three-piece suit, cigarette in right hand, taller than the portly, bald, bespectacled, distinguished older colleague visiting from Germany.

Why this photograph? So the writer, twenty-eight when his father died, apple in some ways fallen far from the family tree, can be reminded of the physical resemblance between himself and his father. Height, weight, mustache. Over time, however, Dr. Pick not only stays in the picture but, slowly, comes more into focus. One day, the writer Googles him. Whonamedit.com describes Pick as skilled scholar and cellist who "served with distinction" in the German army in World War I, "a workaholic…a convinced bachelor," who apparently once said, "'Love is a psychosis which may always be given a good prognosis.'"

Family stories. The writer's father went to Europe in 1922. His father's older brother Marvin, just graduated from Harvard College, won a fellowship to study with phenomenologist Edmund Husserl, and the stipend's dollars were strong enough to support two in postwar Europe. His father wanted to meet Sigmund Freud, then notorious, who'd given lectures in the United States a decade before. In

Germany, however, the writer's father was erroneously told Freud required his students to be doctors, and so began medical studies. Fell in love with pathology. Perhaps met Pick then, or a few years later, completing Harvard Medical School, when he returned to Europe with his young bride, a rising star as leider singer. Nazis coming to power. The writer remembers his mother explaining they were able to get Dr. Pick a Cuban passport in the late 1930s, but he declined to use it, was killed in Theresienstadt Concentration Camp in 1944, several months before the writer was born.

The writer's parents were clear they were Jews, supported various Jewish charities, but refused community pressure to assert Jewishness as the center of their identities. His father, raised in an immigrant household with a father who'd repudiated rabbis in favor of Marx and Darwin, seemed uninterested in anything to do with organized religion, though he lived, without preaching about it, an extraordinarily ethical life. Seemed wryly resigned to the inevitably longwinded presence of the professionally religious at public events. The writer's mother, growing up in a family that observed the Jewish calendar, left Judaism behind with condescension for those who still needed it (this though she made such use of Torah—and Creche— stories in her poetry). Her faith was excellence in art and her bond with her husband. The four children of these parents made no effort to learn more about Judaism, not even as adolescent rebellion.

When the writer came of age, Jews were still outsiders and stigmatized exotics in some fields, parts of the country. There were communities and clubs with restrictive covenants barring Jews, and not for nothing had, say, Kirk Douglas and, later, Bob Dylan, taken Aryan names to advance careers. When the writer was young, more than one Italian-American or Irish-American girl considered him the Other, was tempted to possess and be possessed by such difference —stereotyping the writer could hardly argue with. Fail to return the favor of.

The assimilationist impulse in America seemed to peak in the late 1960s. As it eased, ethnicity again began to be romanticized, several of the writer's Jewish friends, for instance, restoring the family's American name to its East European original. The writer, however, felt no particular connection to things Jewish, knew almost nothing about the Jewish calendar, even the High Holidays. At thirty, asked by a friend in what way, then, he was a Jew, he replied that as far back as fourteenth-century Spain there were secular Jews in the arts who might have resembled him. But that was mostly it, just five or six centuries back, except, of course, for being defined by the curiosities and prejudices of others. He avoided images of the Holocaust, photographic and literary: any one of them—mound of corpses; skeletal survivors—seemed to convey more than enough. Both at Harvard and, later, in California, the writer bumped into the occasional anti-Semite. Had a college friend who could not have gotten his summer resort job waiting tables if his employer knew he was a Jew. And later, in San Francisco, the writer met a rivalrous author who claimed literary authenticity, California born and raised, quick to describe the writer as being "from New York City." Still, this seemed only forlorn, the dead hand of the past.

When, during college, the writer went to Europe the first time, it was less than two decades after the end of World War II. After the murder of half the world's Jews. He and his brother traveled overland to Germany, where his brother was to study, but the writer stayed only several days, uneasy, eager to leave. Even in France, where he settled in, he knew what had happened to Jews during the war, knew about French anti-Semitism, the Dreyfus case. But he liked the language, being in another language, became the welcome guest of a working-class family, met a beautiful, affectionate Danish girl. Everywhere he went in France there were castles. Fortifications, battlements. Carcassone, walls within walls within walls within walls. Many tens of millions had died in twentieth-century European wars—one might have argued Europe was a death cult—but the writer was in love.

In various ways, the writer as hot-tempered college student was, after a dose of some early Anglophilia, increasingly eager to be outside of any history except the record of his own direct experience, making. Stories, credentials: fuck the *Mayflower,* he thought, and who came over on it; fuck the Cohen whose ancestor had been a high priest before the Babylon Captivity. These dice were long since loaded, only left the writer disempowered, envious. In this intemperate defining of the self, the writer was still in some ways his parents' son. Though traditions of music, literature, and science were richly present in his childhood home, there was almost no mention of genealogy, no moral invoked from tribal history. And, by both parents, very strict boundaries were maintained vis-á-vis blood relations. His father a great innovator in medical research and care, his mother a poet fashioning new art, the writer imbibed something of what it was to be self-made.

As reader, the writer was in passionate conversation with authors who'd come before, but to create his own books (had to) set limits on their influence. Otherwise, he'd best become, say, a scholar of Joyce or Shakespeare. Thus relatively free of the past, inventing himself in

California, the writer kept the picture of his father with Pick on the bookshelf across from his desk.

What had come before. Back beyond the extermination of European Jewry, beyond those secular Jews in fourteenth-century Spain who might have resembled him, then back through millennia of begats and begettings of which he was one fruition—thanks to so many couplings, conceivings!—back to Jews excoriated in Torah for consorting with the daughters of foreign gods, as the writer, lover of the exogamous, surely would have done; and back, back to hominids, to fish-ancestors with lungs like ours emerging to breathe on dry land, back to stardust, to the Beginning of It All or Always Was, Big Bang or no. Things and epochs which, never witnessed, seldom entered the writer's mind or art, so much so close at hand and (almost) beyond seeing, describing.

Glenn, friend of the writer from early surfing days, comes by the cottage. Former union organizer, long committed to issues of social justice, he's a Kennedy assassination conspiracy theorist, has spent years investigating and figuring out the whole thing. Zapruder tape a fake; two or three or more Oswalds; inconsistencies in news reports after the shooting as evidence of intentional misinformation. And, so extensive are the deceptions, other Kennedy assassination theorists may be part of the conspiracy. It's all in the book he's just finished. The real story: no one else has come close.

Glenn sits on the loveseat in the living room to have the writer read his manuscript—right then and there, if possible. Has come to talk about the only thing that really interests him anymore, and being deaf in one ear gives him even more trouble hearing what anyone else might be saying. Concerned about Glenn's paranoia—though he has no doubt there was a conspiracy to murder Kennedy, that the truth has yet to be told—the writer brings up James Angleton, CIA spy-master who finally could not figure out who was or was not a mole or double or triple agent. Glenn nods appreciatively: occupational hazard. Then presses on with his monologue inventorying evidence, linkages.

When the writer asks Glenn what's the best that will come of truths revealed in his manuscript, Glenn says that he plans—if not killed by conspirators—to personally deliver a copy to Senator Ted Kennedy, having solved the murder of his brother.

But then Glenn is on to something about the grassy knoll and who killed Officer Tipton. The writer tires. Tells Glenn he won't have a chance to read the manuscript for at least a few weeks. Suggests that if time is of the essence, or if Glenn's life is in danger, why not post the book on the Net. Won't that both get the truth told and remove him from danger?

Not the kind of help Glenn needs. It may be that either one is completely for Glenn's story or one is against him. As they stand at the front door, the writer sees Glenn scrutinize him. The writer hazards a guess at what Glenn's thinking. True, they've known each other for years and years, had so many hours out on the water back in the day. Glenn's aware it's totally fucked to have to confront such a possibility, but that's his mandate, to get through layer after layer of lies. Something, it seems, no one else has the courage, perseverance, or intelligence to do. Think of Kim Philby, double agent for decades. A priori, then, Glen can't assume the writer is not part of the conspiracy.

The writer, mulling. Glenn's no fool, nor is he all wrong. Reluctantly or with zest, writers are always using, exposing, or sacrificing family and friends in the name of a higher loyalty. That thing they call Art. Artists. The writer knew a playwright in his late forties who sold his literary correspondence to a university library for a good price. Perhaps from the start wrote his friends and peers with a subsequent audience in mind.

Literary estates. The writer thinks of his lover in the early 1980s, brilliant young painter who sent the writer hundreds of letters over a three-year period. (Not to mention his to her and their countless, then-crazily-expensive daytime phone calls.) Two decades later he receives a handwritten note from her asking for the letters back, something he'd offered years before. Hoping they'll somehow empower her life or art, though thinking she (too) might have kept carbons, the writer ships them to her, relieved to have them at their proper destination, whatever she has in mind.

"When the now came dressed as then," Edward P. Jones wrote in *The Known World*. Then and now. Before mailing the box, the writer spends a week rereading. What an outpouring! What a courtship, writer being wooed/being shown how to woo, if not in so many words. Or, in so many, many words. Words they shared. "You asked me to remind you in the morning of the word *chasuble*. Thus, beautiful man, *chasuble*." And how the writer celebrated the removal of her vestments!

"An aspect of my being tips in your direction," she wrote, "like a raft on a summer lake when someone sits down next to you." And what scrutiny, this observer who wanted to look at him as no one had before! Noting "concavity of shadow below your ribs, diameter and shade of your nipple, the way it lifts to my lips."

"I want to be right where your sense of wonder begins." She was trying to negotiate the terms of a life together. And for clarity. Early on she remarked that the writer seemed determined to avoid any hint of domestic strife, misunderstanding, erotic rancor. And it was true, in his mid-thirties, newly single, there was much he'd resolved to risk living without. Much he treasured not having to negotiate. Reluctantly, she hazarded that in fact the writer had enough of what he needed without her. A thousand miles apart, both of them possessed by what they were working on and wanting to be possessed by what they were working on, she concluded he was "matching your life to your book's life." As she perhaps was matching hers to her paintings. Savoring the order of her studio as he savored the calm of the cottage, she imagined one day being rich and famous with a *pied a terre* in San Francisco. She'd visit him, but only for a few hours at time, never spend the night.

Rereadings. How much he'd forgotten of their extraordinary exchange. How much he had diminished it—her—in his mind. Why was that, why had he not remembered their time together as *more* than the letters now revealed? Because he'd disappointed her, didn't feel good about it? Because, finally, he'd resolved to curtail their already attenuated contact when he started seeing Serena? True enough, but still the letters left him uneasy. How trust himself as storyteller? And how, with the best of intentions, do justice to what the two of them had shared? To what he'd shared with any of those he'd loved, been loved by? How, really, could one write, knowing there were so many ways to fail?

The landline rings in the cottage: the writer's childhood friend Henry. Knowing each other what, more than half a century? As usual, they talk Red Sox Nation—Papi, Manny, Schilling, Papelbon. And, of course, Steinbrenner's Yankees. Baseball armistice, a DMZ since the run-up to the Iraq war. The writer's intelligent, very generous, responsible old friend. "Weak-kneed," Henry termed the antiwar demonstrators in 2003. Said, of Cheney, "a man of probity." His testiness then sounding to the writer like Bill O'Reilly excoriating "the Left." Writer aware his friend was equally disheartened to hear him so predictably parrot the *Nation's* editorial page. Writer thinking that over the decades he should have been a better friend, somehow saved Henry from his own bitterness.

In the period before the invasion of Iraq, another of the writer's friends—jazz musician in New York, no silver spoon and stubbornly self-made in arduous pursuit of his art—enjoys shocking fellow musicians by saying he's all for war, will vote—again—for Bush. Wants to know what the writer thinks. "Doesn't much matter," the writer responds, dismayed by watching the follies and lies of the Vietnam War inexorably recapitulated. Tired of the country's refusal to acknowledge the nightmarish disconnect between its shameful foreign policy and heroic myth of itself. "Doesn't much matter," he says to his musician friend, "but story suggests I should fear that at some future time you'll be ashamed of yourself." Which makes his truculent friend laugh.

The Bush administration's deceptions, ineptitude. Pathetic strutting of men who cleverly avoided combat. "We won't be fooled again," The Who sang. Wrong: people hunger to be fooled.

How the story really goes. It is written: 1. no solace for the dead and wounded; and 2. long life for Bush, Blair, et al. The writer thinks of Wolfowitz, preening technocrat. Kicked upstairs to the World Bank, too smart for his own good. Such a hoary trope. Remember McGeorge Bundy, cocky genius? Oops, promoted to run the Ford Foundation. "No success like failure," as the poet put it. Time without end for the best and the brightest, like Robert MacNamara, to duck/bob/weave even past age eighty, avoiding full knowledge of what they did. To avoid...contrition. Enough time for terrible truths to seep out, sink in, as with Kissinger, at risk of being put on trial in various countries. Linked forever now to Pinochet. Think of Lyndon Johnson, how quickly he died—willed himself to die?—after not running for reelection, perhaps to avoid MacNamara's Sophoclean fate. Mythic, Johnson's demise, MacNamara's evasions.

Mid-2006. Three suicides in one day by inmates at Guantánamo Bay, deemed by Rear Admiral Harry Harris Jr. "not an act of desperation, but an act of asymmetrical warfare waged against us." Perhaps, the writer thinks, perhaps in the name of fair play the admiral and two colleagues should reciprocate this dastardly tactic. Meanwhile, the writer discerns flickers of understanding in Bush, rich boy so long coddled, if only that he seems unsettled by turning sixty. "The older you grow the worse the discoveries you make about yourself," Bellow writes in *Ravelstein*. Think of the graves Bush has filled! Forget war-crimes charges. Consider the moment in that dead of night when Bush starts counting not sheep but the dead, his dead.

Born-again? Playing with fire, self-aggrandizing stories about the Whirlwind by the self-anointed Elect. One hundred million angels singing, "Golden Ladder / Golden Throne / Kingdom Come"? No. Nope. In his interminable decades after 2008, entourage diminished, dry denier now a born-again barfly, Bush hears late Johnny Cash singing "Revelation" on the jukebox: "Whoever is filthy, let him be filthy still." And, "If they gave gold statuettes, for tears and regrets, I'd be a legend in my time."

But is the writer reading the entrails right? Will the ancient stories obtain? Tales of rue, penitence. (Not for nothing, so many words speaking to one human quality. *Compunction,* for instance, from the Latin *pungere,* to prick or sting. Remorse, also from Latin, to bite again.) But why, why would such stories not obtain? What's new about humans, really? Once more, the writer thinks of the last line of Larkin's "The Old Fools": "Well, / We shall find out."

Finding out: the writer loves the Japanese film *After Life.* Its premise: right after you die, you enter a halfway house where, with the help of staff, you have to choose one moment from your life to depict in a video. Then, taking only that moment with you, you move on to the next life. Those unable to choose their moment remain in the transit station as staff. (Art: admiration can lead to emulation; the writer's often thought of doing his own telling of the film's story. But the next life has just never been high on his list, a kind of focus or myopia engendered by parents so agnostic, or living so fully here and now, that they didn't even mention it.)

Shrive: to impose penance on for sin; to grant absolution to a penitent; to confess to a priest. From—who would have guessed?—Latin, *scribere,* to write. The writer recalls the word from his Shakespeare class at Harvard in 1961. Thinking now that life turns out to be not just what you did but the story you made as you were doing it. Not the story you tell yourself or others along the way, to applause or calumny, but the story when you are finally capable of really admitting it. Not death-bed confession; rather, story that insists on telling itself to you, late at night, late in the day. The one you have to make peace with.

Fate of the earth. Five years earlier, collaborating with marine photographer Wayne Levin, the writer wrote with anger about the human-induced dying of the oceans, argued that only aquariums, those high-tech other oceans, would survive. Now a friend emails him about the imminent "end of the world": global warming. A decade to go. In the meantime, a long and cold—for northern California—winter. Writer thinking the tropics would be kinder to aching bones. Thinking he might have to renovate the cottage against old age.

The Ides of March. More schoolboy knowledge, Boston-style, from back in the day, date predicted for the death of Julius Caesar. But in the cottage, nothing to beware on March 15; it's just dark when the writer comes in from campus, turns on the lights. And there, high on the bathroom wall, is the first crane fly of the year. All six legs intact as it perches, perhaps two inches long, three inches tip of wing to tip of wing. And then that slow bumbling motoring from spot to spot, not inspiring confidence. Picture, say, the first Wright brothers flight.

As for "insect essence," as the writer's mother put it? Different, apparently, from the black flies the writer swatted so mercilessly. Crane flies: during their few days in the adult stage, they live to mate, and their entire life cycle—egg/larva/pupa/adult—is six weeks. Though crane flies seem inept and fragile, and are easily caught, there are

14,000 species in diverse habitats, which suggests they may be less inept than the writer thinks. Than he is, if he intended a comparison.

Crane flies: not quite the swallows of Capistrano, their return to the cottage. And only one so far. The writer tries to examine his affinity for these…manifestations of the Creator. Does he need more data? To know about ovipositor on female abdomen? That crane flies are food for skunks/moles/fish/turtles/birds/bats? Or does the writer believe that, if he pays enough attention to the crane flies, what he needed to learn will be revealed?

Cottage as site of the profane miraculous? This given the writer's capacity to wish himself elsewhere, somewhere…better? Freer? New York City, Honolulu, Paris, the ranch circa 1975. It's said that some people are defined by what they escaped from, some by the fact that they are forever escaping. An escape artist for sure, the writer escaped to…the cottage. Which, manifestation of the life being lived, of the recalcitrance of the quotidian, inevitably has limits. Whatever miracles contained within, the cottage also incarnates the precluded. Is the bed the writer made, sleeps in.

Miracles; beds. An email just arrived at the cottage begins, "Dear Brothers and Sisters in Christ." This would be the writer's old friend Stew—now, after many confused moltings, an ordained minister. Jew who hungered, as he once put it, "to be a blond." Stew: just like everyone else, the writer used to argue, only more so. And, three times, instrumental in the writer's life. In 1968, Stew was working for a new underground paper, brought the (would-be) writer by to meet the publisher. Later, Stew showed the writer's pieces for this paper to a New York editor, who then offered a book contract. The writer's first. A few years later, anti-war activist turned realtor, Stew urged the writer to buy the cottage, throwing in his commission for free and handling the paperwork. Barely convincing the pennywise writer that a thousand dollars plus or minus on a thirty-year mortgage was nothing much to worry about.

Writer in the cottage, ruminating. Not fate of the earth but fate of the self. "How did I get here?" Brother Stew, all Peace and Love, if not hand of the Divine, then surely deus ex machina.

W riter trying out a new story on others, seeing if he can find a way to make it plausible to himself. Tells friends he's clearing the attic, thinking of leaving the cottage. Says this to Kit, Dick's wonderful wife, who seems almost shocked. Kit's children are grown and successful, she's a grandmother, both her parents have died, she's been a writer and editor, she and Dick make annual trips to Europe, go hiking in the Sierras, but seems shocked. Her response leaves the writer wondering, Should he be shocked?

He also tells Serena—at their regular monthly sushi dinner, evoking the weekly sushi therapy they practiced for years together before separating—"I'm thinking of selling the cottage."

"What about your support system here?" Serena observes matter-of-factly.

At home, the writer phones a liquor store in Southern California to order another case of Lagavulin single malt. Once again, the price has gone up. Over the years, the writer's heard several explanations: vastly increased demand, fire in the distillery. "Actually, they may stop selling it at all, just put it in blended whiskey," the store manager now tells him. Which makes no sense—why not simply raise the price as much as they want? On the other hand, why is the writer surprised Lagavulin might cease to exist, he who's saying he's leaving the cottage?

In the study, writer at his computer, again going to File/Save. Writer copying manuscript onto hard drive, printing out hard copy, burning a CD to put in the trunk of the car. Writer: someone who saves text. Saves himself by saving text? And what has manuscript done for the writer lately? Oh, taken him deeper, deeper. But is that saving the writer? Led or misled, the writer looks up from the bottom, suddenly vertiginous when he sees the mirror of the surface far, far above.

The writer's second novel. Not autobiographical, the writer likes to say: pure understatement. Savoring the cottage's "Clear sequence of appetites," Binta feels *The Beholder*'s "female character lingers on in the cottage as a literary ghost…Although small, the cottage feels boundless, to harbor a lofty hidden chamber large enough for a parallel narrative." Madwoman in the attic? Not for Binta. After dinner one evening, she craves the cottage's "radical quiet," asks to stay the night.

Order, calm. The writer reads about a munitions depot in Guatemala, found to contain National Police files documenting kidnappings and killings—"human rights abuses." But why would torturers leave incriminating records, thousands of names classified *disappeared, assassinated, political detainee*. In the *New York Times,* an expert describes the files as "institutional memory…To expect a bureaucracy to destroy [them] is to expect it to commit suicide."

Perhaps staving off some end of something with his own archives, the writer is nonetheless impelled to cull, pare: books put out in the garage/library or given away, last year's student stories discarded. And now, added incentive: Rachel's coming to visit. The cottage will feel smaller, he needs to make room. And to tuck away.

What became of the writer's work with figure models? Planned nonfiction became fiction. When *The Beholder*, his second novel, was published with recurring descriptions of photographs taken of themselves by the protagonists, the writer's friend Phil called with congratulations, then said, "So when do I get to see the Polaroids?"

"What Polaroids?"

"The ones in your locked desk drawer," Phil might have replied, had he known. In *The Beholder*, before again departing, the young woman asks her writer-lover, "But wouldn't the pictures do just as well?"

So, Rachel's due in from New York City. "Living things are drawn to the flame of privacy," the writer once wrote, doesn't ever want to have to make an issue of a locked drawer. Will take the photos to a storage facility. Or, can he—writer, human being—finally destroy the Polaroids, these images of her with him, once and for all.

To *exhume:* humus, earth; to dig (a dead body) out of the ground. When the writer finally again opens the drawer—it has been three years—there she is. There the two of them are. He begins to weep. As Mark Strand wrote, "in/A world without heaven all is farewell./... Farewell no matter what." No matter what. The writer's surprised he's so...invested. Remembers a joke: "Hear about the Buddhist vacuum cleaner? No attachments."

Attached to the max, the writer shaves, studies grizzle and wings of white chest hair in the mirror. Mirrors. The one in front of him on the bathroom cabinet, two small shaving mirrors on a nearby shelf. Full-length wall mirror by the back door, another in the bedroom: simple decoration also amplifying space. Upstairs, tucked away in a closet, one more mirror gathers dust. The writer bought it for salsa practice, but would sometimes carry it downstairs into the bedroom, the better for him and his *inamorata* to savor themselves together. "Oh, look at us," she once cried.

Out of sight/out of mind? What you see is what you get? What you don't see is what you don't have? In that book on Houdini the writer was reading late, he'd marked this line: "The absence of desire and real death, of which the death of desire is a foreshadowing, are the two great hauntings." *Haunt,* from Old French, *hanter,* to frequent, resort to. The memory and ghost resonances are secondary. As for there being two great hauntings, well, the writer thinks, there could be three.

Channel surfing upstairs one evening, the writer comes across a PBS program about Dekyi Tsering, mother of sixteen, including the Dalai Lama. An extraordinarily compassionate woman, apparently, much loved. In the morning, the writer wakes feeling what he terms "contact compassion," wonders how long it will last.

6:30 A.M. Writer eight blocks from the cottage, as usual sitting in his car in the parking lot, sipping a double cappuccino, leafing through the morning papers. Knock on the roof. Bob, beaming.

"Can only stay a minute," he says, "have to feed the cats."

The writer nods. Years ago, Bob started helping to care for the starving feral cats around his workshop down near the Bay. Would trap them one by one, take them to the vet, have them doctored, spayed, neutered, bring them back to the shop. Over the last ten years, seven have survived. Celebrate his arrival each morning, swarming round him, tails held high.

"Have you seen the crow that hangs out around here?" Bob asks. "Only one leg. I've started giving it some of my bagel. Now it waits for me." He laughs, as if at his own impulses. Seventy-two, incredibly robust despite one ailment or another, thorough in researching the maintenance, repair, and renovation of his body—house of his soul!—he talks about retiring, but savors being very good at what he does, the appreciation of clients, architects, and engineers. Likes providing work for his crew. Entertains thoughts of building yet another—one last—house for his wife and himself.

"Have to go," Bob says. To the feral cats, not to be confused with the cats at home. Down at the shop, there's one he medicates every day—steroid on his finger to rub into its ear. "Transdermally," Bob explains. Before this regimen, the poor creature had multiple infections, would lose large clumps of hair. Each afternoon, Bob returns, and then, this cat in his lap, the two of them doze off for an hour or so.

"I groom Philo," Bob says, "and he grooms me."

"Philo?"

"Colette named him, after the town where I used to hang out up in Mendocino."

"Philo? From the ancient Greek."

Bob nods: allowing that's possible, awaiting more data.

"Bob, do you know what *philo* means?"

"No." Said calmly. As if words are the writer's tool and the writer should know how to use them.

"*Philosophy:* love of wisdom. *Philology:* love of literature." The writer thinks of philodendron, refrains from adding it. "The point is, Bob, *philo* means love."

Watching Bob's pickup leave the parking lot, the writer considers how their paths have intersected over nearly four decades. That apartment Bob offered to share in 1972, writer back from North Africa. A stay Bob and his daughter made in the cottage in the mid-1970s, Bob's gypsy period, daughter recovering from an operation. Summer of 1980, when both Bob and the writer stopped smoking: suffered, commiserated, vanquished the demon addiction. Bob picking him up at SFO in 1984 after his mother's long dying. Dinner in 1998 at

Bob and Colette's beautiful home in the country, night the writer's left circumflex artery occluded. Not to mention, now (a cat named) Philo.

Philo. Driving home, like everyone the writer in one and the same moment both living and dying. Having lately undervalued the former, he seeks a return to the wellspring of his love of the world, of narrative. Back in the cottage, picking up Calvino on Italian folktales, he reads of their examination of "human vicissitudes" and "catalog of the potential destinies of men and women,"

> especially that stage in life when destiny is formed, i.e. youth, beginning with birth, which itself often foreshadows the future; then the departure from home, and, finally, through the trials of growing up, the attainment of maturity and the proof of one's humanity...[This] encompasses everything: the arbitrary division of humans...into kings and poor people; the persecution of the innocent and their subsequent vindication...love unrecognized when first encountered and then no sooner experienced than lost; the common fate of subjection to spells, of having one's existence predetermined by complex and unknown forces.

Writer hoping by fidelity to his craft to be restored to his true self. Or, in a variant of an old story, the writer might be asleep in the cottage/castle, now "surrounded by such a vast number of trees, great and small, bushes and brambles, twining one within another, that neither man nor beast could pass through." Having been asleep for years and years, the writer can be restored to a waking life only by a...princess and her kiss.

What have I become? the writer asks. Wondering, given the trouble he has recognizing himself these days, how she'll be able to know it's him.

Katrin calls. Twenty-five years since they separated, fifteen since they've seen each other. Fifteen years: can that be so? They do, however, talk every few months. It's a mean time for Katrin: both parents have died, her rivalrous older sister did her worst in settling the estate, and the fairy tale of family Katrin told herself turned out to be false. Or, she asked the wrong things of her parents, who never did love her in the unconditional way she needed, demanded. Many times the writer urged Katrin to get free of them—the long struggle gave her an air of great remove from the things that occupied most other people—but she could not, nor could she live a life her parents found adequately conventional.

After their deaths, she still had her animals—cats, dog, horse. But now her thoroughbred, a great love—love of her life?—has died. "I thought of marrying the horse," Katrin says, laughing bitterly. "What I had with him was something between *Romeo and Juliet* and *A Midsummer Night's Dream*."

When the writer first met her, Katrin was immersed in the arts—ballet, books, fabric, music. Treasured, at first, that the writer was a writer. Didn't treasure, though, the second of the two books he wrote during his years with her, his fourth. This despite good reviews, fellowships. Too much irony, Olympian detachment. As if in making art of aspects of their struggles he had no stake in solving them. The writer thought her perfectionism was possible because, despite so much talent in so many media, she didn't finish things. Didn't need to finish things? Thought also that about his work she was absolutely right.

Reading Berger's *A Painter of Our Time,* the writer arrives at the title character's conclusion that

> All can heat…[The artists'] privilege, if that is what it can be called, is that we can also cool—with the terrible coldness of our discipline.

"And Jane came by with a lock of your hair..." Line from Leonard Cohen's brilliant "Famous Blue Raincoat," singer emphasizing, articulating her name in a way that leaves the listener unable to forget it.

Jane. More than a year into the book, this book, the writer's read sections to Andrea in the living room and, occasionally, read a few paragraphs over the phone to Chester or his friend Stephen in New York. Now, he asks Jane, perhaps twenty-one, former student who wants the work, to read the manuscript. In the cottage; writer won't let it out of his sight. Colleagues, agent, editor—voices the writer has been willing to hear only after the manuscript achieved the authority of a nearly finished book. He knows, for instance, of a married couple, both authors, proud to say they work in the same office, adjoining desks, show each other everything. Writer laughing to picture this: what can they not allow themselves to think, set down?

Since the writer can sometimes relate to the audience-adverse pianist Glenn Gould, then why Jane of all people? Well, in seminar she was over and again insightful in her critiques of other students' work, is clearly a lover of story, very much a would-be writer. In some ways still a naive reader and, the writer thinks, a hard sell. Which is good. Unsure of what he's achieved, wondering if this particular self-portrait of the artist will dismay others (is it unsettling him?), the writer decides he better risk the idealism of the young. (In "Closing Time,"

Leonard Cohen sings, "And I lift my glass to the Awful Truth/which you can't reveal to the Ears of Youth…")

Arriving one morning, Jane chooses the loveseat in the living room as her workspace. After three hours, they sit at his desk and go over the first fifty pages, Jane doubting she's bringing much to the task, though it turns out she's picked up lots of typos and punctuation errors. Good work, the writer tells her. He's most interested, however, in two notes she's made. In the opening story, you'll recall, about the attic and three plagues, the writer counts on testimony of creatures he's guided safely out of the cottage "to help him avoid being turned on a spit over burning coals for ever and ever." And in the margin of the second story, where the aloes may someday "blackmail the writer, be called on to testify against him," Jane writes, "The writer's crimes, what are they?"

Jane's set to return in a week to continue reading. Will perhaps find the answer to her question in the text. And what does the writer hope for from her? Well, that she continue the good work of copyediting. That she further interrogate what the writer's up to. That she, in the end, admire both book and author. And what more might one ask of Jane? Only that…that…she become a writer, one day publishing a story about a young woman curled up on the loveseat in the living room of a former professor. Dictionary close at hand. Working her way through his manuscript about life in the cottage while he's at the computer in the adjoining study, at that very moment writing about why he chose her as his book's first—and perhaps perfect—reader.

"The summer after my heart procedure," the writer says, commencing a story twice-told, "I was fifty-four. Strange period. I was still processing what had hit me, and it seemed likely I'd have to go back for another operation. Maybe thirty-five percent of the time that's what happened. Clint Eastwood as Dirty Harry, robber staring up at him and his .357 Magnum, which may or may not have one round remaining, says to the robber something like, 'You have to ask yourself, Do I feel lucky?' Well, I didn't feel lucky. But otherwise I felt fine—exercising heavily, eating almost nothing, had lost my appetite, was thin, lean. Everybody told me how good I looked.

"Anyway, one day my old friend Nora and her clan, down from Tahoe, showed up at the door of the cottage. Her husband, Ron, their three teenage daughters, her former lover, Arthur—bohemian ghetto gangster now suddenly in his seventies—and Nora and Arthur's grown daughter Venus, my god-daughter. The whole mispoche, as they say in Yiddish. Once more I felt great admiration for Nora. Fertility-goddess feminist, belly dancer, lover of unguents and potions, astrologer able to specify each person's array of qualities while never mistaking aspects for the whole. Perennially buoyant lamenter. When Nora separated from Arthur soon after Venus's conception (Nora had of course consulted the stars for the best moment), she kept him part of the family after he returned from a stint in county jail, welcome frequent visitor. Venus's dad. Long since, Arthur and Ron were good friends.

"Over the years, whenever Arthur phoned me, he'd begin, 'Hey, Thomas, ol' stick, what's shakin'.' And always I'd reply, 'Ain't nothing shakin' but the leaves in the trees.' 'Leaves' taking forever, as if out of Amos 'n Andy. Usually we'd have a moment of silence for Arthur's old companion Suede Jackie, so-very-dapper black dope dealer from back in the day. Epitome of outlaw charisma, style. Four blond wives living together at his farmhouse in Marin back then. Now, however, still in prison.

"Anyway, that day in the cottage, there we are in the living room, and I notice that Ron, informed consumer of sensimilla and cocaine, has one eye that keeps blinking. I figure since he'd put on a lot of weight and was drinking too much, perhaps he has some kind of ocular problem. Nor can I give him my full attention; I'm being bombarded with conversation. It was like the old days in the cottage, teeming, lots of laughter. But then I notice Ron again, eye still blinking, but now he seems also to have some kind of tic—his head keeps yanking toward the kitchen. Finally it dawns on me: Ron wants to meet me there. I get up and go around one way, Ron the other. As we both arrive at the stove, I see he has what we children in Boston used to call a shit-eating grin, and there's a vial out of which he's tamping a thick—massive—line of cocaine onto his index finger, which is already beneath my nostril, which is already power-inhaling, snorting up the entire enormity.

"And immediately, that so-familiar nasal drip down the back of my throat, promise of impeccable neon clarity. Ron—6'4" and just south of three hundred pounds, hippie botanist as well as longtime pacifist—rocking back and forth on his heels, very pleased, now generously laying out a redwood-trunk of a line for himself. Then pointing at the living room, forefinger to his lips. Shsssh: family's down on his drug and liquor use; he's supposed to be reforming.

"All of this was so familiar, but in truth it had been forever since I'd snorted cocaine. Almost twenty years, despite never having paid for it and many fine all-nighters. I'd just left it behind. Preferred pickup basketball. Still, talk about reflexes! I didn't miss a beat when the line was offered. But now, now I suddenly come back to the present, realize that snorting cocaine shortly after a heart procedure is, as they say, contraindicated. Fuck! It wasn't like eating, you couldn't put a finger in your mouth, puke what you'd mistakenly consumed. What to do? I stood there looking at Ron, who was beaming satisfaction, my mind working with a kind of hyper-clarity, cool remove from the mundane with an overlay of fond memories of impeccable cocaine wordplay and the prolonged erotic.

"'Good, huh?' Ron asked. I studied his food-stained shirt. My so-very-kind purveyor and, possibly, hulking and hirsute angel of death. What a fucking way to go!

"'Great,' I heard myself answer, and it was. Fantastic, actually.

"Ron motioned again toward the living room. Right. Social obligation, and he had to beat it before he got busted—one of his teen-age daughters was really down on his dissipations, ashamed of her old man.

"Back in the living room, Arthur was telling stories of the old days: his two Great Danes, his turquoise and silver and suede boots, how he would hit on hippie chicks until he met his match in Nora. Summer of 1967.

"In the cottage that day, late afternoon became evening, and eventually Nora and her clan departed for a rock concert. Out on the street as they drove off, I shook my head, wondered at the wonder of it all, felt lucky, actually, to have been reminded of both my friends and the power of this amazing—life-threatening?—substance. And then, awfully tired out, I went back to the cottage, slept.

"Of course, the ensuing weeks I worried I'd done myself in, but felt no adverse effects. At last, several months later, to my great surprise the doctor gave me an all clear. That was eight years ago. Make of it all what you will."

And what does the writer make of it all? Well, story, obviously. "Jus' twenty-one and don' mind dyin'" kind of story; braggadocio, death defied. Talismanic, such narrative, regaining control of folly. Writer also making survivor story, writer still here, Arthur dead and gone. Further, story not just to please but to instruct, to argue about how we—all—are. Writer as moralist, moralizing. And, just once, in this version, shaking the ridgepole of his story to find what he now makes of it, the writer sees Nora's extended clan as an asterim, cluster of stars, apparently random celestial grouping it was his pleasure and fate to behold, be part of.

A mile from the cottage, the cornucopia of Peter's bookstore. Brilliant seller of first editions and, in typical acts of generosity, publisher of two beautiful letterpress chapbooks of the writer's work, Peter also has a gift for correcting the writer in the name of improving his character. Stopping in at the shop, the writer tells Peter about his current project, this book. Peter snorts. "You've always come and gone when you wanted. Teaching and surfing in Hawai'i months at a time, not even knowing if you'd ever return, extended trips to New York, fellowship in Fiji." All this is factually correct; Peter has it no less than half right. If the writer's immersion in the cottage has been deep while in residence, he's also been away a great deal—often had, as they say, one foot out the door. (Or, one foot on the platform, one foot on the train.)

The writer considers trying to convey something about what the cottage means to him, but Peter, still in front of his computer, papers in his lap, is, typically, impatient to get back to work. *I'll just show him the book when it's done,* the writer tells himself, thinking such an option is one really good thing about the written word.

Getting out of his car when he reaches home, the writer sees eighty-two-year-old AO, self-described "cognitive analyst" striding strongly down the street, wild turkey feather in Australian bush hat. The writer spots AO all over town, always on foot, striding strongly, and they exchange waves, sometimes offer each other a joke. AO

perennially jaunty, grizzled, garrulous, quick-witted, ready to be
amused, always a cardboard sign on his back:

Talk about any
ISSUES OR PROBLEMS.
I will listen.

Heading through one gate and then another, once again reaching
the aloes and front steps, the writer's cheered. If the book, this book,
proves too much for him, he can always find AO, tell him about life
in the cottage. Make AO his role model, leave Chaucer behind.

"Hey, you. You in the cottage. Waiting for something?"

"What if I am?"

"Or, is it somebody? You seem to have all the things you need."

"Except immortal life, perfect health, and, like everyone else, 20% more money. Still, stipulate that I do."

"Then, you need somebody."

"'Not just anybody.'"

"Beatles. But you have lovers, or women who want you to be their lovers."

"'Can't help it if I'm lucky.'"

"Dylan. But you're holding out for someone special."

"And if that's the case?"

"A last great love. Chatelaine for your castle?"

"Who told you that?"

"The aloes."

"Mind-reading pieces of shit."

"Sorry. But, really, do you think at your age that's likely to happen?"

"You tell me."

"I mean, you 'don't get around much anymore.'"

"Ellington."

"And you're 'not half the man you used to be.'"

"Beatles. Still, as Chester said at eighty, 'all the parts still work.'"

"Congratulations. But, you're not afraid of being alone?"

"Like everybody, just less so. Somewhat more stubborn, and foolish. Next question."

"Think you'll find her?"

"'Any day now, any way now.'"

"Dylan?"

"Who also wrote, 'It's not dark yet, but it's getting there.'"

Not dark yet. But, long since, intimations. Writer thinking back to 1965, finally good at the game of college, utterly not ready to push on to whatever was supposed to come next. Phi Beta Kappa/Magna Cum Laude, dope smoking, belatedly and increasingly bohemian, and…just wanting to drift. But how to do that? Down to New Haven in late August that year, law school the era's default setting for the unsure. Dropped out and back to Cambridge within ten days. Immediately, saved!—into grad school in English lit. Then realizing—he was very young for his age—that grad school was not at all about The Meaning of Life or, even, Art. Was a "profession," much required credentialing, pronto.

Before the writer quit grad school en route to further floundering, he lucked into a seminar on Hemingway and Faulkner. So much of that year is a blur, or obliterated. He cannot for the life of him remember why he fought with his Virginia Woolf–obsessed girlfriend—now dead, he recently learned. ("Orgasms of twenty years ago leave no memory," says the narrator in Elizabeth Hardwick's *Sleepless Nights*.) Nonetheless, the writer can still see his marvelous, Eurocentric roommate Joe laboriously preparing squid, or Joe in the bathtub, chino cuffs at his knees, box of detergent in hand, stomping his clothes as if they were grapes in a *vendage*. Strange: the writer recalls the name or face of not one fellow student in that seminar, but easily summons an image of the professor in his belted, multi-buckled, too-continental trench coat. Is embarrassed to remember asking the professor, then in his late thirties, thin, thin-lipped, prematurely bald…could the writer have been asking what the professor imagined he had in common with Hemingway?

As for the seminar's material, of course the writer doesn't forget the maudlin finale of *The Sun Also Rises,* no doubt also absorbed some of the novel's technique. Still, few of Hemingway's stories or characters stay with him, displaced by the writer's impression—never read biography!—of Hemingway as self-pitying bully. As for Faulkner, the writer retains an impression of an avalanche of words, books—*Light in August; The Sound and the Fury; Absalom, Absalom*—that were so seductive an incantation he never revisited them.

Nonetheless, over the next four decades one particular scene comes to mind every year or two, unbidden. And no, not Popeye's corncob rape. *The Mansion,* published several years before Faulkner's death, when he was struggling with alcoholism and various injuries, concludes with the demise of Mink Snopes. It is this passage the writer at long last (and something like Faulkner's age when Faulkner wrote it) rereads:

> In fact, the ground itself never let a man forget it was there waiting, pulling gently and without no hurry at him between every step, saying, Come on, lay down; I aint going to hurt you. Jest lay down.

Mink does lie down, to give the ground the chance to "prove what it could do if it wanted to try":

> [A]s soon as he thought that, it seemed to him he could feel the Mink Snopes that had had to spend so much

of his life just having unnecessary bother and trouble, beginning to creep, seep, flow easy as sleeping; he could almost watch it, following all the little grass blades and tiny roots, the little holes the worms made, down and down into the ground already full of the folks that had the trouble but were free now, so that it was just the ground and the dirt that had to bother and worry and anguish with the passions and the hopes and skeers, the justice and the injustice and the griefs, leaving the folks themselves easy now, all mixed and jumbled up comfortable and easy so wouldn't nobody even know or even care who was which anymore, himself among them.

So this is what the writer remembers! But now, after so long, he finds—of course?—that Faulkner wasn't finished:

> [E]qual to any, good as any, brave as any, being inextricable from, anonymous with all of them: the beautiful, the splendid, the proud and the brave, right on up to the very top itself among the shining phantoms and dreams which are the milestones of the long human recording— Helen and the bishops, the kings and the unhomed angels, the scornful and graceless seraphim.

The writer smiles: pure Faulkner, inducing a high he'd had to work to come down from when he started to write fiction. But it's also true the orotund finale of this long sentence isn't what most registered on the writer when he was twenty-one. No, it was just "unhomed" Mink giving it up, deciding to lie down on the ground.

Unhomed. Seven years later, at twenty-eight, the writer made a rocky reentry from months in Greece and North Africa. End of a six-year relationship he'd been far too slow to end, forced his lover to end for them. Dislocations and cutting of roots that were apparently imperative, taking him someplace…he had to go. Again back in California, sharing Bob's apartment: porch room with yellow blood roses below the window, mattress on the floor, desk a massive unfinished section of redwood burl Bob had milled on Jenner Beach. And that month-long spring flu they both had. Perhaps, staggered in so many ways, the writer became able to see some things more clearly.

Several years later, now at home in the cottage, Katrin dancing in the living room, he set down a story that became part of *Who Wrote the Book of Love?* (1977):

> Though surely they were always all around me, I never saw them until the end of a rainy winter, and really not until early one evening when at long last the sky cleared. And then, in the afterglow of the waning day, they came into my ken, came out like stars. An elderly woman walking home from market, pausing after achieving a block before attempting the next; two aged gnomes, him with cigar pulling the wife behind; a grandfather watching his heirs mortgage the home he paid for free and clear. And Rose. "Once an adult, twice a child," she cackled as she watered her garden, throwing snails out into the streets. Her six cats watching.

This to introduce his character Rose, inspired by the eponymously named Flora, who had a garden on a vacant lot near Bob's apartment.

> Anemone, crocus, marigold, primrose, iris. ("Iris makes you believe in God, doesn't it," she said.) Hyacinth, fox-glove, tigridia, gladiolus, scilla, hollyhock. Black tulip, Johnny-jump-up, nasturtium, sweet william, columbine, verbana, phlox. Campanula. Cosmos. African lily, regal lily, black lily of the Nile. Canterbury bells. Snapdragons. Bird-of-paradise. Forget-me-nots.

All the notes the writer took at Flora's garden, before, during and after his long flu, dizzying return to the United States. (The day he arrived, seeing his long hair, the attractive female customs agent in Kennedy Airport had asked, alluringly, "Got any dope?") The writer's great hunger to be able to name what was in Flora's garden: rereading the story thirty years later, the writer knows he never once thought of saving Flora, but did intend to try to do her justice as he used her for his own purposes. Carefully recreated both the universe of her garden and diction of her confusions, losses, sorrows.

In the cottage now, the writer puts down *Who Wrote the Book of Love?* thinks, *I'm the only person surprised by how old I am.* Remembers Cicero's question, "But what can be more in accordance with Nature than for old men to die?" Which puts the writer in mind of the epigraph, from Nietzsche, for his seventh book, his third book of stories:

> My formula for the greatness of a human being is *amor fati:* that one wants nothing to be different, not forward, not backward, not in all eternity. Not merely bear what is necessary, still less conceal it…but love it.

Hence *Learning to Love It.* Dispassionately omniscient author suggesting that, willy-nilly, you'd be loving it all the way…down.

So: now that the writer's future has fewer hypotheticals remaining, less room left for correctives, what was he thinking back in his late forties when he invoked Nietzsche? Of course he had aches and pains—gum surgery, sciatica, meniscus problems, reading glasses for the first time—but was still more or less himself, person he'd been since, say, graduating college. Roughly same height/weight, same face in the mirror plus or minus a wrinkle or two. Or ten. But did the writer think he was going to live forever? No, no: never any such thing. But neither did he imagine real change, an end of his life. Not that this failure of the imagination took intention; the word *denial* doesn't catch it. This was an effortless presumption of an ongoing something-like-the-present, continuum of more or less the same self. Ever becoming—evergreen!—while, of course, needless to say, "getting older." How easy it was despite, for instance, being at the hospital watching his mother's inexorable decline. Or despite seeing the lava fields and flow on the island of Hawai'i, made too aware of a time eons ago when land was first created. A time before humans, obviously.

Anyway...want to know something really funny? Imagine the writer's surprise when it all dawned on him! Hilarious! Odd, perhaps, it didn't occur to him when his left circumflex artery closed, in ICU or coming home after surgery: this seemed only a form of harassment he'd have preferred to duck. Maybe, seven or eight years later, after more of the tumult of love and work he'd clearly been born for, a shoe finally dropped. Late-April Taurus in the bullring, mounted picador at work, matador at the ready. Not a fair fight.

Thus edified, the writer weighs the consolations of philosophers:

> Again, suppose nature should suddenly lift up her voice, and herself rebuke some one of us in these words: "Why is death so great a thing to you, mortal, that you give way excessively to sickly lamentation? Why groan and weep at death? For if the life that is past and gone has been pleasant to you, and all its blessings have not drained away and not been enjoyed—as if poured in a vessel full of holes—why don't you retire like a guest sated with the banquet of life, and with calm mind embrace, you fool, a rest that knows no care? But if all you have reaped has been wasted and lost, and life is a stumbling block, why seek to add more—all to be lost again foolishly and passed away without enjoyment? Why not rather make

an end of life and trouble? For there is nothing more which I can devise or discover to please you: all things are ever as they were."

Lucretius. The writer particularly likes him ventriloquizing Nature, having Her say, "all things are ever as they were": nice mysterioso reverb. But as for the two and only two alternatives that Lucretius/Nature sets out? The writer's reminded of a technocrat famous in his day married to his friend Dora. An early feminist male, eager to share in the domestic, though of course his time was valuable, Dora's husband would manfully man the barbecue at their parties, laying out great hunks of steak, had a gift for defining the terms of argument from behind a chef's apron. "Understand," he'd admonish with percussive conviction, looking the writer in the eye from under his toque, employing the always-inveigling hortative. "Understand there are three ways to think about this," such testerone'd enumeration launching his argument into the category of the half won.

Rhetoric. Ol' Lucretius knew his Aristotle. Knew argument wasn't synonymous with truth. Knew Nature might not have seen death as…as clearly as Lucretius had Her see it.

Serena's son Billy, now twenty-two, his summer fighting fires with a crew from his university. Boots with very thick soles, camaraderie, good pay, months camping in the wilderness. Trying "smokeless tobacco" while there (writer fighting not to say something about baseball players and cancer of the throat and mouth). Back in town after Labor Day, Billy totals his car: leaning down to pick up his cell phone, apparently, he swerves, loses control. Car a total loss, Billy unscathed. At least four or five lives remaining. Eager to finish college, meanwhile, he plans on taking an extra course this semester. And though he could afford another used car with savings from firefighting, his current game plan is to commute by bike to classes and his girlfriend's.

Clearly a work-in-progress, but no more or less so than the writer at his age, Billy inquires about the cottage book, the writer's work-in-progress, seems to be asking if it's a good idea to spend so much time thinking about death, mortality, last things. "But that's my job description," the writer replies, "it's what I'm paid to do." Wondering, hearing these words, if they're true, a white lie, or just plain false. Maybe, he thinks, I'm laying out a map for the future, guidebook for the duration. Or maybe I just believe there's power to be had with this material, can't resist a run at it. "It goes without saying." A writer: someone unable to go without saying.

Being sixty-two. You'd think some possibilities are long since fore-closed. But: sister of a friend, nearly forty, wants to collaborate on having a baby. And Rachel, Lower East Side struggling artist, late twenties, suddenly finds herself dreaming of having a child, asks the writer about his availability. Meanwhile, a friend of the writer, sixty-one, wife in her early forties, just had a second child, couldn't be more happy. Hard to tell time with these new biological clocks…

Because of his part in raising Billy, the writer has a pretty good sense of what childrearing requires. Demands. Also, he long ago came to the conclusion that people who really need children just have them, find them. Over the decades: a woman acquaintance, no mate, full-time job, adopts one Chinese girl, then another; a woman friend consults the stars, gets pregnant by a lover about to go to prison, has the baby, goes on welfare (later marries someone else, has two children with him as well); an ambivalently single male friend marries his best friend's widow, helps raise her infant daughter; a male friend marries a woman with two sons, raises them as his own, has a daughter with her.

The writer's also long believed that no one gets to do everything in this life, and that writing books is a choice, an expensive one. So in part, having children or not has seemed related to having time and money to be able to do his kind of books. Author Evan Connell, the writer recalls, said—savoring hyperbole; expressing fear?—that he never had a family because he "didn't want to end up bagging groceries in a Safeway." The writer has a neighbor, sixty, grateful for his much younger, vibrant wife and bright, healthy, athletic four-year-old daughter, who nonetheless yearns for the space and time to get to his next book project. And this, the writer concludes, is a state of being he avoided. Though like everyone he can be of two minds, the writer seems decisive enough about devoting his best resources to the books that need, as some people can't refrain from putting it, to be "born." (Whatever the difficulties of gestating and birthing text, the writer's never mistaken a book for a baby. This though both before and after publication, a book may seem like a child threatened by illness, or very difficult teenager putting himself in jeopardy.) *Withhold:* to keep back, refrain from granting, refuse. From *with* and *hold?* But how? Ah, Anglo Saxon *wither,* against. All that the writer withheld in holding books so dear.

So, that's it for kids? Well, as a marijuana-smoking/marijuana-smuggling friend of the writer used to like to say back in the sixties, "You jus' never know." Who would have thought, when the writer was in his mid-fifties, that he'd be starting a novel about an older man and much younger woman who, trying to describe what they were to each other, would come to feel she might be both wife and daughter?

Paul Simon: "This is the story of how we begin to remember." As if you wake one morning and they (they?) remove the blindfold (*blindfeld,* Middle English, struck blind). As if your story's a relentless bounty hunter who finally apprehends you, takes you back. As if scales fall from your eyes. In the conversion of Saul-become-Paul on that road to Damascus, Saul, hunting Christians, is literally blinded by the light when Jesus addresses him. Spends three days without sight (though his eyes are open). Ananias, after Jesus appears to him in a vision, goes to Saul and lays hands on him. "And immediately there fell from his eyes something like scales: and he regained his sight forthwith…"

Struggle, sin, redemption, personal growth. Our hunger for such tellings must be in the genetic code. The writer, however, resists conversion stories, has met too many of the multi-/re-/deconverted. Heard of too many memories recovered only to be reconsidered, repudiated, debunked, "forgotten." Still, there is always at least "the other side of the story" to consider, though, the writer wonders, just where exactly might that be?

Nightfall. Winter storm. The cottage hears the writer on the phone. He's talking with his old friend Ruby about her son Stan, multitalented former outlaw, now, since her gift of a small home and rural land, fairly domesticated and, occasionally, tranquil. Still a well-armed survivalist kind of eager for Armageddon, but hard at work renovating buildings, raising purebred dogs, making more babies. A real homestead, the cottage thinks, enviously. Home place.

Wallace Stevens: "The house was quiet because it had to be." The cottage: reserved, self-contained, self-effacing. Long-suffering: knows it will never be the subject of one of those rhapsodic bestsellers about the author's life-saving/life-changing estate in Tuscany. Cottage aware the writer's unfaithful, despite Bob's renovations back in the day, recent "twenty-five-year" roof, periodic repaintings of clapboard, trim. All very practical. But where's the love? "And what," the cottage again asks, "what about those French doors in the downstairs bedroom that were to have opened onto a redwood deck in the yard? Or raising the roof, which would have doubled square footage, added a bathroom, an upstairs balcony for sunbathing? And need I mention the shower downstairs?" No, the writer's commitment has never been complete, cottage for him in some way perennially makeshift. A substitute, the cottage broods, but for what? Knowing the writer (inevitably?) returns to order and clarity he seems unable to (bring himself to) establish elsewhere. Not to mention, the cottage barely refrains from adding, when the cottage's been not just workplace and shelter but—in the writer's darkest hours—life-support system. "You know I've always been there for you," the cottage continues. "Where's the justice? And, if you don't mind my saying so, what about what happened to Lear when he gave up his home? Not very pretty, was it?"

Late that night, the storm strengthens. Cottage sighs. Moans. Shudders. Roused from fitful sleep, the writer thinks of something for his book. Gets up, goes into the study, turns on a light, makes a note on a filing card: *The rest of my life.* Is sure, without elaboration, that it will lead him somewhere in the morning. Then, chilled, the writer goes back to bed. "Stop the hectoring," he says to the cottage as his head hits the pillow. "Wheedling, whining, whinging. Leave me alone." Is not sure, as he nods off, whether or not the cottage retorts, "House: rhymes with...spouse."

Morning. Synonyms, antonyms, homonyms/homographs/homophones. Categories as if never not grasped from infancy on in a home where language was play, shield, art, weapon. For example: *wrest, rest, rest.* Wrest: wrist; wrestle. Rest: No rest for the weary. I rest my case. Laid to rest. But also, with no suggestion of repose, the rest of my life.

"No baggage," common desideratum in Personal Ads late in the last millennium, part of the very human search for mates free from the entangling past. Back in town, the writer heads out to the garage-library, surely baggage car on the train of his life. Browsing, he pauses at the epigram and death alphabet (adjoining the sex and erotica alphabet). Because a few epigrams go a long way—he'd rather write than read them—some of these books he took a taste of, gleaned something from, set aside. Now, *The Silence of the Body* again catches his eye. More than once, the writer's had his mind expanded by Ceronetti's insights, humor:

> The main risk of cunnilingus is forgetting the person on whom it is performed, since the act immerses the devoted practitioner in pure Shakti, in the immortal sign of the Mother, in the infinite waters of Maya…swallowed by the waters, the lover loses sight of the woman's face and name.

Pleased to be cautioned while advised to conceptualize the act as philanthropic—another *philo* for Bob!—it occurs to the writer that seeing the garage-library after two months in Honolulu made him smile, and the Ceronetti has given him…joy. Where would he be without it? Or what?

Home and away. The writer's rediscovered his slippers under the bed downstairs. As if he'd never been gone. In Hawai'i, he worked on his cottage book—this book—without having intended to do more than light editing and reading. Having assumed that as usual he'd defer to, submit to the ocean, allow it the space and time to restore him yet once again. Up as always before dawn that first morning in Honolulu, however, he did not head downstairs to the surf rack in search of morning glass, surfing's state of grace. Instead, coffee/the desk/the manuscript. As in the cottage. That in Honolulu the writer did so day after day, week after week, undercut his intimacy with ocean, now a lover thwarted, importuning, his book's rival. Writer reminding himself it had been forty years since joy or quest had been experienced free of the possibility of being alchemized into words on the page. Sometimes, essential hours of writing done, the writer would study the breaking waves, the deep blue, the horizon. Feeling, disconcertingly, that it all was sheer, finished, two dimensional, an oil painting. No longer offering a point of entry.

Writing it was. As, perhaps, it had always been. And reading: *Anna Karenina* in Honolulu, lugging the tome around to cafés, writer chastened by Tolstoy's compassion for his many characters. Paramour of Art having renewed his vows, the writer was both moved by the novel and eager to see what he could take from it. Not for himself, exactly: for his book.

Again in residence in the cottage—high and dry!—the writer goes around around the corner. His friend Ella, accomplished writer, works in a small trailer in his neighbors' driveway. She and her husband live in the hills, but, more resolute than she lets on, Ella keeps this modest workroom, all her own.

"And your cottage book," Ella says, "I can hardly wait to read it. Are you done yet?"

ousesitting in New York City. Friends have given the writer their spacious loft while they're away; he's beneficiary of their aesthetic, years of renovation. Of course no home—structure or house of self—is without flaw. Here, however, the writer will not have to deal with, say, the leaky parapet (Latin, to guard the breast, hence a "dwarf" protective wall).

Down five flights, on SoHo's cobblestoned Ganges, hordes of weekend pilgrims sport cell phone/iPod/cigarette/sunglasses, tote huge shopping bags and, underarm, dogs the size of newborns. Women in remarkably skinny skinny jeans, seven-league boots clip-clopping like horseshoes, men in avian- or Renaissance-inspired frippery as they window-shop, drift, dodge a curb-jumping bike messenger, skirt enraged honking black Lincoln Town Cars going nowhere. Pilgrims: negotiate sidewalk gridlock at Spring and Broadway, ferret out/try on/model; unfurl hundred dollar bills, charge. Styling, manifesting themselves to mirrored selves, manifesting themselves also in the eye-mirrors of others crowding, jostling. (Humans forget names, not faces.) Pilgrims, gorging. What insatiability! What faith in beauty, in possessing. No ontological confusion here: everyone on the street knows what they want, chant or text-message the mantra—MORE.

Five flights above the sirens and consumption's siren call, the writer practices his own forms of greed. On endless repeat Cecilia

Bartoli sings a heartrending Giordani song, *"Caro Mio Ben"*: "My dear love,/at least believe me..." Writer simultaneously lovelorn in the Italian eighteenth century and editing this manuscript. Perusing his friends' bookcases, he spots Easwaran's translation of *The Dhammapada*. Finds another rendering of the passage Bob had given him in Fat Apple's a year and a half before, when the writer had been describing the cottage's renovations and three plagues:

> I have gone through many rounds of birth and death, looking in vain for the builder of this body. Heavy indeed is birth and death again and again! But now I have seen you, house-builder, you shall not build this house again. Its beams are broken; its dome is shattered: self-will is extinguished, nirvana is attained.

Cuban exiles who knew Fidel way back when have written that he could not dance. So: did the Buddha not shop? What he...desired, for himself and others. A real person, probably five centuries before Christ, the Buddha becomes fairy tale, as he perhaps intended. How his story goes: Prince Siddhartha, living within the walls of the royal estates, in his late twenties is finally allowed to go out into the world his father-the-king sought to insulate him from. Sees for the first time someone ill, someone old, someone poor, someone dead. Horrified, Siddhartha's not consoled by dancing girls his father provides to cheer him. That night, courtesans asleep, Siddhartha concludes their silks and makeup are only the tinsel of appearance, part of the "strange illusion," Easwaran writes, "that makes us believe the beauty of the moment can never fade." Inspired by the ascetic holy man he'd observed out in the world, Siddhartha resolves "to go forth from the life he had known, not to see his family again," until he finds a way to move beyond aging and death. Takes that getaway male's last look at sleeping wife and child. Buddha the renouncer dropping out, declining ordinary life, the householder's "squalid exigencies and mean quarrels," as Carrithers puts it. Henceforth on the road, in search of what as the Buddha he later terms "the unborn, the unageing, undiseased, deathless, sorrowless, undefiled supreme surcease of bondage." Finally, eighty and soon to die, he tells his disciples—no doubt anticipating they'd fight for possession of his ashes—"remember, all things that come into being must pass away."

Buddhist diction. Rejecting the world of misery and sorrows. Transitory. Subject to decay. Destruction of desire. The cause of sorrow, the way to escape from it. Awakening. Transformation. Liberation. Salvation.

The cause of sorrow. House the writer grew up in: walnut paneling and banisters; tiled front hall; music room with two pianos and walnut cabinets holding sheet music and scores; large vestibule (three-syllable sounds the writer loved as a child). Superbly maintained, the house was clean, in order, secure. How did his mother do it—raise four children, write, perform, care for her husband? Amazing. But still, the house was no walled estate. And despite parents who were aristocrats by merit, the writer, though well protected, lived in the world as they wanted him to. His father's hand on his forehead when he was ill, yes; his father's respectful colleagues eager to care for the family. Lessons, overseen by the writer's mother, abounding. But also, trudging in "galoshes" to grammar school—public school—after a winter storm, old man down on the icy street, blood on fresh snowfall. Around Boston, any meandering child on the trolleys or in subway stations would behold so many unremarked-on human gargoyles. Hunchback, dwarf, cripple, blind newsboy. Drunks, the bleary, the beleaguered. Lots of buck teeth: not much corrective dentistry then. Worn colonial-era structures or a Puritan graveyard's Tower of Pisa–like stones spoke not only of longevity but of lives long lost. The gravity of history: Boston then a city in decline. New England death trip—there had been lots of passings-away by the time the writer was a child.

Closer to home, the writer's mother contracted tuberculosis at eighteen, right after marrying, survived years of semi-invalidism. The writer's father nearly died in his mid-forties, required a long convalescence. Longwood Towers, a nearby apartment-hotel, removed him from the tumult of four young children. Subsequently, for his remaining two decades their father struggled with his health while continuing his mission. That pioneering hospital for children with cancer he dreamed and built was, in the early years, where the children were cared for and, in many cases, where they died.

The writer's junior year of college, not yet having taken on the austerities of writing (akin to the extreme mortifications Siddhartha practiced, then repudiated?), rock 'n' roll on the car ster-e-o, he drove west, away, away from his version of the fallen world Siddhartha discovered at twenty-nine. Arriving, finally, in the Golden State: Great God Almighty, the space, light, bounty, mobility, freedom! Apartment with pool! Oh, it seemed to the writer there was no death in northern California.

No death. This conclusion required a certain myopia on the writer's part: his summer job, for the State Department of Public Health, was to interview a sample of people who'd "lost" a family member the previous year.

Writer at his desk. Leafing the pages of Canetti's *The Secret Heart of the Clock,* just in from the garage-library, he finds an aphorism that makes him stop. "He who has too many words can only be alone."

Writer—on his own, as they say—poring over a draft of several new epigrams. Still incredulous he became entranced by the form a decade before, set out to write some, then to make a chapbook, another chapbook, and finally a book of them. Did. And, now, amused he seems to want to persist, though the epigrams' brevity brings him (perilously?) close to silence. Giving the epigrammist, but perhaps also being, the last word.

Old man, difficult, complaining, dying. Unbecoming.

Young woman. Making out but not consummating. Near Miss.

The man who could do almost anything for himself, French-kissing her.

For though the light of these Fires and Tapers be not so natu-
rall, as the Moone, yet because they are more domestique
and obedient to us, wee distinguish particular objects better
by them, than by the Moone.

JOHN DONNE

S ex. Love. Birth. Death. The big monosyllables. House. Home.
When the writer was growing up, in a fit of "redevelopment" the
city of Boston razed the West End, put in the Southeast Expressway,
replaced a thriving neighborhood with residential towers. Advertis-
ing the new apartments, there was a sign by the adjoining, rush hour-
jammed freeway ramp. Half a century later, the words come back to
the writer.

IF YOU LIVED HERE YOU'D BE HOME BY NOW

The end of March, when each of his parents died. In California this late winter, an unusual month: record endless rain, none
of the familiar high blue clearing between storms. No sun—tough
for a heliotropic writer. Just beyond the front steps, however, across
from the aloes, the calla lilies are exuberant. Beautiful showoffs. Pure
white funnels and cones: spathes. Each tight embrace unfurling to
reveal a long yellow spike: spadix. Perennials, the calla lilies, endur-
ing, everlasting, transplanted by Katrin thirty years ago. (About the
aloes. It's not quite true the writer did nothing for them. Over the
decades, many a night he's gone out to study moon or stars, stood on

the doorstep, and, neo-Luther Burbankean having read that urine is nourishing nitrogen, bestowed his benison on the aloes.)

Writer in late winter. Rhetorical questions. What's a book worth? Or, what's a book cost? Or, what would have been the cost of not doing the book? How run the numbers? Writer mulling, imperfectly remembering someone's line: "What a price the gods exact for song, to become what we sing."

Cottage. It finally occurs to the writer to look up the word. Old French, *cote,* hut. Of course: dovecote. Also coterie, once an association of landholding peasants. The writer then looks up coffin: longshot. Nope, not related. But maybe it's the book about the cottage that's his coffin? Which sounds grim—a dead end!—until the writer remembers Queequeg's coffin and Ishmael-the-storyteller's survival because of it. Though, head shaved for so many years, and after so much wandering in the South Pacific, the writer's loath to drown his inner Queequeg.

High wind, downpour drumming on Bob's skylights. Not long before dawn, cottage pitch black, headphoned writer up to pee. Autopilot: left at bedroom door, then straight ahead, pushing bathroom door. Return with right turn at bedroom, drifting left until contact with bedframe, then into (controlled) tumble. Once more under five heavy blankets, plumping the pillows, the writer remembers Larkin's "Groping back to bed after a piss." Hums a line from The Pogues' "Fairy Tale of New York"—"the boys in the NYPD choir were singing 'Galway Bay.'" Lets it go. Gone.

Up at six, by 6:30 back into…this manuscript. Nothing having intervened since being at his desk the night before except sleep and, as they said when he was young, "calls of nature." Weeks now of again showing up for the book each new morning, everything mandated by the writing rhythm. Book and self coterminous: bordering, sure, but also having the same ending? The writer thinks of "My Grandfather's Clock," so popular in his childhood, stopping "short, never to go again, when the old man died."

And what's happening? Writer finding himself in/losing himself in the book? Giving in to the book? The eros of writing. Read all about it—Writer Fucks Book. Book Fucks Writer. Or perhaps, the writer thinks, perhaps the book's like warm ocean, both nurturing and threatening. Or, on bad days, the manuscript's a viral parasite, writer the host. At this moment, however, the writer reads it as the woman with whom he's dancing. Artistic vanity: he taught her the moves, how to get her groove on. But now, each leads and backleads the other, music of words calling the tune.

Patience with process, with self. This ongoing rhythm, centering. Like breathing. Like deep breathing. Calming, yes, but not unambiguous. The writer again thinks of his daily ocean swims in Honolulu. Breaststroke, slow and steady: face in water, long exhale; pull, face up, strong inhale. Hypnotic, as one heads away from shore. Always a surprise, the no-doubt-inevitable impulse to return.

Thrall, from the Scandanavian, Icelandic: one who's in bondage, enslaved. *Enthrall:* to subjugate; captivate; hold spellbound. And *spell,* verb transitive: to name or write the letters of a word. *Spell,* noun: a form of words possessing magic power, an incantation, enchantment. *Chant:* to celebrate in song. Writer: in thrall to, enthralled by, his mother tongue, seeking to…cast a spell. Writing itself a kind of trance. State of profound abstraction: ecstasy, rapture, musing. Two quite different worlds being mediated.

Writer in his study. Searching the row of his mother's books, pulling down *House Hold Poems*. Its epigraph his mother's translation of a poem by Nelly Sachs:

> In my room
> where my bed stands
> a table a chair
> the kitchen stove
> the universe kneels as everywhere
> to be redeemed
> from invisibility

So: cottage (more) visible. Once, at his favorite surf spot near Diamond Head, children on shore playing in the backwash, the writer realized the obvious: they'd be riding waves long after his ashes were strewn out on the face of the deep. When he'd return to the break—if ever, if at all—as...warm rain. "Dead as a doornail," idiom of the writer's Boston childhood, apparently traceable on the page back to the fourteenth century. And surely worth carrying into the future. Belatedly, now, late in the day the writer wonders who will be in the cottage when he's gone.

Till then, however, rewriting: interrogating; flensing, expanding. Manuscript if not less misguided, more nuanced. Increasingly precise language better exposing flaws of design, author's character. Writer grateful for his patience, stamina. Text a rock face, writer-climber finding fewer and fewer points of purchase. Meanwhile, busy-busy, as Vonnegut put it, he's thinking outside the box: hey, cannibalize these nonfiction stories for use in a novel. Writer aware it's easier to picture a different book than to labor on the one at hand, that any genre allows only an aspect of the true. Still, to—nobly!—sacrifice the manuscript in favor of some putative greater good has appeal.

Writer remembering Updike's argument that Melville stopped working in prose not because of falling sales and bad reviews but because he'd expended all his narrative capital. What, if anything, to save for later? The writer has black dress shirts he has to force himself to wear to salsa clubs: too beautiful to diminish by use.

'Nother huge problem: sun's out. Surely the book was inflected by the interminable rain winter, writer bleak, bleaker. The despond of waking into darkness. Now, basking in the yard, shirtless and sporting polarized Oakleys, squirrel scurrying up the jasmine, hummingbird hovering, jay screaming…taking this in, the writer's certain an easier winter would have made a less melancholy tome. Lying in the sun giving the lie to what he felt was true. All right, then, he'll add a disclaimer: *This book was written under the influence, the duress, of…*

Gamely pushing ahead with what is, the writer weighs "Winter's Tales" as subtitle. Takes stock of benefits and costs of the third-person singular. Though it's the voice that's written the book, still, the writer has an appetite for more of the first person. Just itches to say "I." Such decisions are important, ever more so. "I mean," the writer tells himself, sun baking, oh, baking sternum/thigh/skull (Norwegian, *skol*, shell of egg or nut). "I mean, Tommy, get a grip. The end's in sight. This could be your last book."

"Too true," the writer replies, "but you come from Boston. Yankees sweeping five from the Sox at Fenway? All songs are swan songs." Swan songs. Which makes the writer recall the common taunt of his childhood, "You look like death warmed over."

Death warmed over. One morning, he wakes thinking, *Let the dead bury the dead.* Goes to his New Testament. In Matthew's telling, Jesus says to a disciple, "Foxes have holes and birds of the air have nests, but the Son of Man has no place to lay his head." Then another disciple says to Jesus, "Lord, first let me go and bury my father." To which Jesus replies, "Follow me, and let the dead bury the dead. " In Luke's version, a disciple says, "Lord, I will follow thee; but let me first go bid them farewell, which are at home at my house." And Jesus responds, "No man, having put his hand to the plough, and looking back, is fit for the Kingdom of God."

Tough love. No farewelling? No looking back? The writer agrees: He, Jesus, had it absolutely right. But he-the-writer, life in lower case, isn't thinking about the Kingdom of God. His calling's the here-and-now, all about farewelling. Burying the dead. And, for that matter, some of the living.

Selective writer's block. Clearly against his will, so to speak, after years of berating himself the writer finally comes up with a revised Last Testament and Directive to Physicians. No such resistance, however, with this manuscript: the writer's been eager, driven, to see what he had to say, still worships the god of completion. Also, as Doctorow put it, "You live enslaved in the piece's language, its diction, its universe of imagery, and there is no way out except through the last sentence."

Sunny September, Indian summer kind of feeling. Writer thinking about Amma, saint-like woman from India who's embraced more than twenty million people, sometimes twenty thousand in a single day, offering unconditional love, inner healing. A word-warrior, the writer likes the notion of a nonverbal spiritual experience, purification by hugs and embraces, a sweet smile. No (inevitably disputatious) texts.

Late afternoon, having again reworked the section about the lover whose letters he returned, the writer's done for the day. Waiting, meanwhile, to hear what Ella, his second reader (after his former student Jane), thinks of the manuscript, but she's at a performance of Chinese opera. Writer in the living room, finding in the *New York Times* that Sylvester Stallone, speaking of his diminished career, says, "An artist dies twice, and the second death is the easiest one."

"Maybe," the writer mutters. Just then comes a stentorian shout

from the gate: Philip, self-diagnosed paranoid schizophrenic, very verbal, acute reader of others, quick to violence, quintessence of Boston
Irish lumpenproletariat, inspiration for the writer's recurring character Mad Dog. They sit in the yard, Philip inhaling one beer, another,
writer marveling at Art reincarnated as Life. Sixty now, white haired,
Philip had disappeared for seven years before this manifestation.
Philip still unfalteringly himself—loud, relentless, sensitive, reveling
in sagas of barroom combat, capable of honest self-appraisal. Nearly
forty years since they first met, in this regard he is utterly reliable.

Philip. A bear hug, and he's off down the street. Gone again. Back
in the cottage, the word *reliquary* surfaces in the writer's mind. Re-
pository or receptacle for relics—surviving memorials of something
past, things kept in remembrance. Clearing his desk, the writer feels
very, very close to the end of the book, can imagine parting ways
with it. An embrace, then the book heading down the street?

"What I meant to say." Writer turning back to his desk, making a
note of it, repeating the idiom to himself, sensing he might want to
make something of it. Then thinking, Time for scotch and almonds.
On his back on the bed upstairs, head propped on several pillows, in
a state of single malt–induced contemplation, the writer again looks
out at cedar and acacia, squirrel and jay. "Act your age," he tells himself, recalling the stinging admonition of his childhood. Wondering
now exactly what part that means he should play.

Sipping and munching, the writer reminds himself, I have to call
Bob. Tell him about Amma and Philip. End the book with something about Bob.

Epilogue

Reprise: a repetition, return to an earlier theme. Which, given changes in perspective over the years, might be experienced as something startlingly new. Young Jade Piano, 碧琴, "home" again after a day out in the world, emerging from the tub. Entoweled. Smiling. Eyes dancing. Writer at bathroom door, right hand on white doorframe, staring at—trying to memorize—her. Thinking...*etymology:* the "blood" in "blessed." Two months since they met. One e-ter-ni-ty, two e-ter-ni-ty...

In the front yard, the largest aloe (*Agave attenuata*, the writer's belatedly learned) has sprouted a thick arching shaft, now twelve feet and still surging. A once-in-its-lifetime—twenty to sixty years—massive inflorescence. Monocarpic, the aloe will die after this sole blooming.

碧琴, tub behind her. "What?" she teases, hands opening the towel, then, quick, closing it, as if in self-defense. Laughs. Pretends to pout.

Long pause, writer processing what the eye glimpsed. *Revelation:* the miraculous, disclosed.

Vertigo: time-traveling, writer sped—blasted—across decades lived before 碧琴 was even thought of, born.

Where were we? Where are we? Yes: right hand; white doorframe. The cottage, bathroom, 碧琴, towel.

"Are you ready for bed?" the writer asks her, hearing the idiom as if for the very first time.

Acknowledgments & Author's Note

Many thanks to Andrea Camuto, Sara Bershtel, R. T. Denton, Anthony Dubovsky, Ella Ellis, Fran Kaufman, Helen Lang, Starling Lawrence, Bik Lee, Laura Glen Louis, Pat Matsueda, Stephen Mitchell, Sam Otter, Brian Peterson, Stephen Rosenberg, Michael Sierchio, Frank Stewart, Max Track, and Andrea Young.

Nonfiction and veracity: various names and métiers have been changed (to protect the innocent, as they used to say), but nothing recounted here is otherwise factually untrue. Why, however, these particular truths among so very, very many—well, always a fair question.

Berkeley • Honolulu • New York City • Paris • 2005–2008